BARRON'S

NORTHERN BREEDS

Margaret H. Bonham

²CONTENTS

MEET THE NORTHERN BREEDS

The Northern breed dog is any dog descended from the ancient line of spitz-type dogs with pricked ears, thick double coats, almond-shaped eyes, and a tail that curls over the back in some fashion. Most people tend to think of these dogs as "wolfy" looking. Spitz-type dogs are usually more independent and stubborn than other breeds. Their desire to work is strong, as is their energy. Rugged and adaptable, they have been man's guardians, transportation, hunters, herders, and companions for thousands of years.

The History of the Northern Breeds

No one really knows when the first dogs were domesticated. Archeologists originally placed the domestication of the dog between 10,000 to 20,000 years ago. However, new evidence suggests that Man's Best Friend dates back 135,000 years. This research traces mitochondrial DNA mutations and concludes that man domesticated the dog when he migrated from Africa. Further DNA study supports the dog's direct descent from the wolf. This research also suggests that many different wolves contributed to the dog's ancestry and to obtain more desired traits, humans occasionally crossed wolves back in.

The Norwegian Elkhound is a Northern breed dating back over 5,000 years.

The Northern breeds history and ancestry is not clear, given current research. Many modern-day Northern breeds—the Alaskan Malamute, the Canadian Inuit Dog, and the Chow Chow—date back beyond records of written or oral history. Many experts believe that the spitz may have developed from pariah dogs mating with indigenous wolves, but DNA research suggests that there was no one group of wolves or dogs that founded particular breeds or types. Most likely, interbreeding between dogs existed before humans settled on one "type," and bred for those qualities.

We do know that various Arctic peoples did settle on a tough spitz-type dog capable of pulling sleds or sledges, guarding the home, herding, or hunting. Each environment required special adaptations. The Sami people of Lapland required a dog that could herd reindeer; the

Mahlemut people required a dog that could pull heavy loads and hunt polar bear. The Chukchi required a fast dog, capable of hauling moderate loads over long distances; the Ainu required a dog capable of hunting and guarding. Each time, the spitz-type dogs were able to adapt and perform the roles admirably.

In North America, Native peoples had used the dog for thousands of years as a mode of transportation in the upper Midwest, Northeast, Canada, and of course, Alaska. Fur trappers and mail carriers were two of the first groups of Europeans in the Americas to use sled dogs and the Northern breeds for transportation, but sled dogs were an anomaly. This changed when gold was discovered in the Klondike in 1896.

The Gold Rush

After 1896 dogs played a crucial role in bringing men and supplies into the Klondike. Malamutes, Canadian Inuit Dogs, and other indigenous dogs filled the role admirably, but they were too few. Dogs were in such demand that many were stolen from Seattle, San Francisco, and Los Angeles. Any dog larger than a spaniel wasn't safe. Dogs were also bought and sold, usually for very high prices. These newcomers often intermingled with the native Northern Breeds and helped produce such breeds as the Chinook, the Indian Dog, the Alaskan Husky, and the Mackenzie River Husky.

Exploration by Dog Sled

Into the early twentieth century, explorers used sled dogs in both the Arctic and Antarctic. Robert Peary, with Matthew Henson, successfully led an expedition in 1909 to the North Pole, where he used sled dogs—mostly Malamutes and Canadian Inuit Dogs (Greenland Huskies)—as a means of transportation.

During the same period, 867 explorers attempted to reach the South Pole, most notably Robert Scott and Roald Amundsen. Scott chose to use ponies rather than dogs, although he did have some dog teams present. Roald Amundsen used Northern breeds and reached the South Pole first.

Admiral Byrd led expeditions into Antarctica using sled dogs and tractors. His sled dogs came from Canadian Inuit stock, Alaskan Husky stock, Alaskan Malamutes, and some wolf-husky mixes. The Chinook breed appeared during these expeditions.

Dogs descended from various expeditions still inhabited Antarctica until 1992 when a ban on nonindigenous animals went into effect. Canadian Inuit Dogs were brought from an Australian Antarctic station to Minnesota, where they and their descendants now work in tours.

The Popularity of Sled Dog Racing

Sled dog racing reached a height of popularity in the early twentieth century. One of the most famous races was the 204-mile (328-km) All-Alaskan Sweepstakes in Nome, which ran each year from 1908 to 1917. Siberian Huskies made their debut in the United States in the 1909 All-Alaskan Sweepstakes.

The two most famous Alaskan sprint races, the Fur Rendezvous in Anchorage and the North American in Fairbanks, started in 1946 and continues today. Many mushers took dogs out of Alaskan villages and established a breeding program to create their own versions of the Alaskan Husky. Gareth Wright, for example, bred Targhee Hounds, Irish Setters, Gordon Setters, Indian Dogs, and Siberian Huskies to create his own line of Aurora Huskies, a line of Alaskan Huskies that persists to this day.

The most famous race, the Iditarod, started when Joe Redington, Sr. saw that dogs and mushing were dwindling in Alaska, and the Iron Dog or snowmobile was rapidly replacing the sled dog. Redington started the Iditarod in 1973 to promote the sport of mushing; this race quickly spawned interest in sled dog racing. Sprint, distance, mid-distance, and stage racing all grew because of the Iditarod publicity.

In the lower 48 states, sled dog racing started with the American Dog Derby in Ashton, Idaho, in 1917. Most participants of the American Dog Derby ran hound crosses rather than Northern Breeds, including the Targhee Hounds, which were Staghound-Irish Setter crosses. These Targhee Hounds, now more or less extinct, were crossed into the Alaskan Husky to add speed. Other races appeared in Truckee, California, and Laconia, New Hampshire. Dogs raced in New England included Alaskan Malamutes, Siberian Huskies, and Chinooks.

The Serum Run—
The Greatest Race of All

Perhaps the most famous race was not for money or fame, but against time to save lives. In 1925 diphtheria struck Nome. The city had dwindled to about 2,000 with a population that was mostly Inuit and Native American. Since airplanes were still unreliable in Alaska, the governor sent a relay of dog teams from Nenana to Nome. The feat took just seven days and a dozen dog teams in terrible conditions that included windchills in excess of −70°F

(21°C), temperatures below −60°F (15°C), blinding whiteout blizzards, and sea ice that threatened to break up. Again, Northern breeds, including Alaskan Huskies, Siberian Huskies, Alaskan Malamutes, and Inuit Dogs proved their worth. One dog, Balto, made famous by the children's movie, has a statue erected to him in New York's Central Park to commemorate the bravery of both mushers and dogs.

The Northern Breeds—
Descriptions

Ainu (Hokkaido) Inu

✔ Registration available: UKC (Northern Breed).

✔ Size: Males 19–22 inches (48–56 cm); females 18–20 inches (46–51 cm); weight 35–65 pounds (16–29 kg).

✔ Coat and colors: Double coat, sheds twice yearly; brindle, red, white, fawn, black, or light brown.

✔ Lifespan: 10–15 years.

✔ Health problems: Hip dysplasia.

The Ainu or Hokkaido is an ancient breed dating back some 3,000 years in Japan. These dogs are medium sized when compared with the larger Akita Inu or the smaller Shiba Inu. Named after the native people who lived in Northern Japan, these dogs were primarily used for hunting brown bear. They were declared a Natural Monument in 1937 along with the Akita. They are rare in the United States.

Ainus are intelligent, loyal dogs with a strong guarding instinct. Their coats enable them to live outdoors and make good watchdogs. They are

Akita Inu

Alaskan Husky

fiercely loyal and protective, but should never be aggressive toward humans. Ainus have an extremely strong prey drive and may kill small animals unless raised with them as puppies.

Ainus do well as outside dogs, because they are well suited to colder climates. However, they prefer to be with their owners. They are intelligent and become bored easily. They will focus their boredom on destructive activities such as chewing inappropriate objects and digging. They are active dogs that need daily exercise.

Akita Inu

✔ Registration available: AKC (Working) and UKC (Northern Breed).

✔ Size: Standard—males 26–28 inches (66–71 cm); weight: 100–130 pounds (45–59 kg); females 24–26 inches (61–66 cm); weight: 70–100 pounds (32–45 kg).

✔ Coat and colors: Double coat, sheds twice yearly; any color including white, brindle, or pinto.

✔ Lifespan: 8–12 years.

✔ Health problems: Low thyroid, hip dysplasia, elbow dysplasia, PRA, autoimmune diseases, bloat, pemphigus, and sebaceous adenitis.

The Akita is a Japanese breed whose history goes back to the 1600s when a famous nobleman, exiled to the northernmost province of Honshu (Akita), bred large dogs for hunting and dogfighting. Known as Matagiinu or esteemed dog hunter, the Akita excelled in hunting bear, wild boar, and deer. Only nobility were allowed to keep and breed the Akita and consequently it nearly became extinct several times over the next 300 years. When the Japanese Government declared the breed a Natural Monument, preservation of the breed followed. After World War II, servicemen brought Akitas to America and helped establish the breed in the United States.

Akitas are intelligent, loyal dogs with a strong protective and guarding instinct. They should never be aggressive toward humans, but may often show aggression toward dogs of

Alaskan Klee Kai

Alaskan Malamute

the same sex. They are very dominance-oriented, like many Northern breeds, and owners must establish themselves as Alpha early on to prevent confrontations. Akitas have an extremely strong prey drive and may kill small animals.

Akitas do not do well outside, although they are well suited to colder climates. They prefer to be with their owners. These dogs are intelligent and become bored easily, focusing their boredom on destructive activities such as chewing and digging. They are active dogs that need daily exercise.

Alaskan Husky

✔ Registration available: None.
✔ Size: 20–26 inches (51–66 cm); weight: 35–75 pounds (16–34 kg).
✔ Coat and colors: Double coat, sheds twice yearly; any color or pattern.
✔ Lifespan: 10–15 years.
✔ Health problems: Zinc dermatitis, low thyroid, epilepsy.

The Alaskan Husky is not a formally recognized breed, but rather, a breed that has evolved from bloodlines out of Athabascan and Inuit Alaskan villages and Alaskan mushers' kennels. Often called "mixed breeds" by registered purebred mushers, these dogs excel in every sled dog racing venue including sprint, mid-distance, and long distance. They can be traced back many generations to famous mushers' kennels.

Alaskan Huskies are classified as either Husky or Hound. Husky types look more like traditional Northern breeds. Houndy types often have flop ears and more greyhound-like builds. These dogs can be traced back to Greyhounds, Salukis, Borzois, German Shorthaired Pointers, Labrador Retrievers, Gordon Setters, Irish Setters, and other nontraditional breeds. Alaskan Huskies have a variety of personalities, but all have the overwhelming desire to run and pull. Some are "shy"; others are people-oriented. Most are hyper, have strong prey drives, and an irrepressible pack mentality.

Alaskan Huskies can live either indoors or outdoors, if they receive enough attention and exercise. They are intelligent and become easily bored. Alaskan Huskies will focus their boredom on destructive activities, digging, and escaping. They excel in backpacking and are eager sledding workers.

Alaskan Klee Kai

✔ Registration available: UKC (Northern Breed).
✔ Size: Standard—15–17 inches (38–43 cm), Miniature: 13–15 inches (33–38 cm), Toy under 13 inches (33 cm); Weight: 10–20 pounds (4.5–9 kg).
✔ Coat and colors: Double coat, sheds twice yearly; black and white, gray and white, wolf gray and white, red and white, and all white.
✔ Lifespan: About 15 years.
✔ Health problems: Luxating patella, cryptorchidism, undershot jaw.

Linda Spurlin in Wasilla, Alaska, developed the Alaskan Klee Kai (KLEE-ki) in the early 1970s. They resemble miniature Alaskan Huskies. She bred an undersized Alaskan Husky to Alaskan Huskies, Siberian Huskies, American Eskimo Dogs, and a Schipperke to create the Klee Kai. There are less than 1,000 total dogs registered.

Alaskan Klee Kai's are active, but should never be "hyper." They need a moderate amount of exercise, make good watchdogs, but generally do not bark excessively. They are suspicious of strangers and need socialization when young or they may become shy. Unlike more independent Northern breeds, Klee Kais need attention. A Klee Kai will follow his owner around the house.

While Klee Kais are hardy dogs, they should never be left outside. An unhappy Klee Kai will demonstrate his displeasure by escaping or destructive behavior. However, this is not a good breed to spoil as they quickly become dominant and snappish.

Alaskan Malamute

✔ Registration available: AKC (Working) and UKC (Northern Breed).
✔ Size: Males: 23–28 inches (58–71 cm); weight: 75–120 pounds (34–54 kg); females 22–25 inches (56–63.5 cm); weight: 65–100 pounds (29–45 kg).
✔ Coat and colors: Double coat, sheds twice yearly; wolf-gray and white, wolf sable and white, Alaskan seal and white, black and white, red and white, blue and white, silver and white, sable and white, and white. White is the only acceptable solid color.
✔ Lifespan: 10–15 years.
✔ Health problems: Hip dysplasia, elbow dysplasia, low thyroid, zinc dermatitis, chondrodysplasia, PRA.

The Alaskan Malamute is an ancient breed that came from the Inuit Mahlemut tribe that lived in the upper west part of Alaska. These Inuits required heavy sledge dogs to carry loads across the Arctic. They frequently used these dogs to hunt polar bear as well as for family companions. Alaskan Malamutes played a crucial role in the Peary Antarctic expeditions and worked as pack and sled dogs for the 10th Mountain Division in World War II. The Alaskan Malamute today still works as a sled dog, packing dog, and companion.

The Alaskan Malamute is a friendly, outgoing dog. He is not a "one-person" dog and should never be aggressive toward people. He makes a poor watchdog and guard dog, although his size is a deterrent. This is an independent breed, and while capable of much love and affection, does not follow his owner around.

Unless raised with cats and other pets, Malamutes consider them small prey. Some Malamutes are dog-aggressive and must be socialized with other dogs when they are young. They are also very pack-oriented and may challenge their owners for dominance.

Alaskan Malamutes can live either indoors or outdoors, if they receive enough attention and exercise. These intelligent dogs become bored easily, focusing their boredom on destructive activities, digging, and escaping. They excel in backpacking and while slow, are eager workers in sledding.

American Eskimo Dog

✔ Registration available: AKC (Non-sporting) and UKC (Northern Breed).
✔ Size: Standard—UKC —Miniature and Standard. Miniature: Males 12–15 inches (30–38 cm); females 11–14 inches (28–36 cm). Standard: Males: 15+ –19 inches (38–48 cm); females 14+ –18 inches (35.5–46 cm). AKC—Toy, Miniature, and Standard. Toy: 9–12 inches (23–30 cm); Miniature: 12–15 inches (30–38 cm); Standard: 15–19 inches (38–48 cm); weight: Standard: 20–40 pounds (9–18 kg); Miniature: 11–20 pounds (5–9 kg); Toy: 6–10 pounds (2.7–4.5 kg).
✔ Coat and colors: Double coat, sheds twice yearly; white or buff.
✔ Lifespan: 10–15 years.
✔ Health problems: Luxating patella.

The American Eskimo Dog or "Eskie" appeared in the United States in the nineteenth century. Known as the American Spitz, they were often found with German immigrants and were probably descendants of the German Spitz, the white Pomeranian, the white Italian Spitz, and the white Keeshond. In the late nineteenth century into the early twentieth century, these dogs were popular in circuses as trick dogs.

The American Eskimo is not as independent as other Northern breeds and are very intelligent. The Eskie requires constant attention from his owner. However, good socialization is necessary or he may become fearful and snappy. Eskies are normally reserved and suspicious of strangers. Unlike most Northern breeds, they make good watchdogs. They can become yappy and may be prone to excessive barking.

Eskies make poor outdoor dogs, as they must spend time with their families. Bored Eskies will put their intellect to use as escape artists if their owners do not exercise them. They can also become destructive chewers. They need moderate exercise, compared to other Northern breeds, but need plenty of activities. They are well suited to agility and other sports.

Canadian Inuit (Eskimo) Dog or Greenland Dog

✔ Registration available: UKC (Northern Breed).
✔ Size: Males 27 inches (68.5 cm); females 25 inches (63.5 cm); weight: 66–95 pounds (30–43 kg).
✔ Coat and colors: Double coat, sheds twice yearly; white, brown and white, gray, gray and white, red and white, black and white.
✔ Lifespan: 10–15 years.
✔ Health problems: Chondrodysplasia.

The Inuit Dog is an ancient breed that the Inuit used for hunting and pulling sleds. They were used in expeditions to the North and South poles, and until 1992 Inuit Dogs were used at an Antarctic station. This breed may go back as far as 4,000 years. Some Inuit Dog

American Eskimo Dog

Canadian Inuit Dog

breeders believe the Greenland Dog and the Inuit Dog are the same breed.

Inuit Dogs are pack-oriented and dominance-oriented. They are working dogs and need more activity than most Northern breeds. They are destructive diggers and chewers, are friendly to people but are dog-aggressive with a strong prey drive. Although Inuit Dogs do not bark and are not good watchdogs or guard dogs, they are vocal and they howl.

Inuit Dogs can live indoors or outdoors, if they receive enough attention and exercise. They are intelligent and become bored easily, focusing their boredom on destructive chewing, digging, and escaping. These dogs excel in backpacking and while slow, are eager workers in sledding.

Chinese Shar-pei

✔ Registration available: AKC (Non-sporting) and UKC (Northern Breed).
✔ Size: 18–20 inches (46–51 cm); weight: 45–60 pounds (20–27 kg).

✔ Coat and colors: Harsh coat; solid colors and sable.
✔ Lifespan: 10–15 years.
✔ Health problems: Entropion, ectropion, hip dysplasia, auto-immune diseases.

Although the Chinese Shar-pei's ancestry is virtually unknown, most agree that the Shar-pei and the Chow share a common link, if not ancestry, making this an unusual member of the Northern breeds. Shar-peis are most likely the product of spitz-type dogs bred with Tibetan Mastiffs. The Communists eliminated these dogs in China, but the Shar-pei thrived in Hong Kong and Taiwan. In 1973 a Shar-pei enthusiast in Hong Kong appealed to dog breeders to save the Chinese Shar-pei and interest in them dramatically increased. Today, the Shar-pei is a well-established breed.

Shar-peis are quiet and reserved; some are shy, but many are affectionate with their own families. They are highly independent like other Northern breeds, stubborn, and can be difficult to train. They make good guard dogs

Chinese Shar-pei

Chinook

and good watchdogs. They can be dog-aggressive with a strong prey drive, so they should never be left alone with small pets.

Shar-peis are not outdoor dogs. Their need for socialization requires that they stay with their families. A Shar-pei without constant human contact may become standoffish and aloof. They need a moderate amount of exercise, comparing them to other Northern breeds, but may become destructive if bored.

Chinook

✔ Registration available: UKC (Northern Breed).
✔ Size: Males: 23–27 inches (58–68.5 cm); females 21–25 inches (53–63.5 cm); weight: 50–90 pounds (23–41 kg).
✔ Coat and colors: Double coat, sheds twice yearly; tawny (light honey to reddish-gold) with black markings.
✔ Lifespan: 10–15 years.
✔ Health problems: Hip dysplasia.

The Chinook is a rare breed, stemming from a single ancestor, a famous sled dog owned by Arthur Walden. Chinook had a Greenland (Inuit Dog) Husky mother and a sire that was part Saint Bernard and part Mastiff. Walden bred his leader to German Shepherd Dogs, Belgian Sheepdogs, and Greenland Huskies, producing offspring that resembled his famous dog. Chinook accompanied Walden to Antarctica on a Byrd expedition where he disappeared at age 12, presumably to die alone. The Chinook breed continued after Walden's death, but dwindled to only 11 breedable dogs in 1981. Due to the diligence of the Chinook breeders, there are currently over 400 Chinooks.

The Chinook is a tireless working dog. He excels at pulling sleds and backpacking, but is also a family dog. Although protective, the Chinook should never be aggressive. This is an independent breed. Unless raised with cats and other pets, Chinooks consider them prey. They are also very pack-oriented and may challenge their owners for dominance.

Although Chinooks are capable of living outdoors, they need to stay with their families.

These dogs are intelligent and become bored easily. They will focus their boredom on destructive activities, such as chewing, digging, and escaping.

Chow Chow

✔ Registration available: AKC (Non-sporting) and UKC (Northern Breed).
✔ Size: 17–20 inches (43–51 cm); weight: 50–70 pounds (23–32 kg).
✔ Coat and colors: Two types of coat: rough and smooth; both are double coated and shed twice yearly; red, black, blue cinnamon, and cream are the only acceptable colors.
✔ Lifespan: 10–12 years.
✔ Health problems: Entropion, ectropion, hip dysplasia, autoimmune diseases.

The Chow Chow is an ancient breed used by the Chinese for hunting, guarding, herding, and pulling. Its exact origin is unknown, but many believe it is related to the Samoyed and the Tibetan Mastiff. The Chow Chow is depicted in an ancient relief, establishing the breed as at least 2,000 years old.

Chows are quiet, dignified, and reserved dogs. They are one-person dogs and can become aloof and snappy if annoyed. They are highly independent and are stubborn, making them difficult to train. They make good guard dogs and good watchdogs. They can be dog-aggressive and have a strong prey drive, so they should never be left alone with small pets such as cats.

Chow Chows do not make good outdoor dogs. A Chow that does not have constant contact with his owner may become standoffish and aloof. They need a moderate amount of exercise, comparing them to other Northern breeds, but may become destructive if bored.

East Siberian Laika

✔ Registration available: UKC (Northern Breed).
✔ Size: 20–25 inches (51–63.5 cm); weight: 40–55 pounds (18–25 kg).
✔ Coat and colors: Double coat, short to medium, sheds twice yearly; white, red, gray, gray and white, black and white.
✔ Lifespan: 10–15 years.
✔ Health problems: Hip dysplasia.

The East Siberian Laika was bred to hunt large game such as bear, deer, moose, and reindeer. Like his counterpart, the West Siberian Laika, he was also used to pull sleds in Siberia, although his main purpose was as a hunting dog. The East Siberian Laika made his appearance in the 1800s when Russians selected various indigenous Siberian dogs to produce a hunting dog.

Although wolflike in appearance, this Laika is trainable when compared to other Northern breeds, but he requires consistent training. Unless raised with cats and other pets, ESL consider them prey. They excel in obedience, hunting, and agility competitions.

Although ESL are capable of living outdoors, they need to stay with their families. These dogs are intelligent and become bored easily. They will focus their boredom on destructive chewing, digging, and escaping.

Eurasian (Eurasier)

✔ Registration available: UKC (Northern Breed).
✔ Size: Males: 21–24 inches (53–61 cm); weight: 50–70 pounds (23–32 kg); females: 19–22 inches (48–56 cm); weight: 40–60 pounds (18–27 kg).
✔ Coat and colors: Double coat, sheds twice yearly; all color-permitted except white, liver, or white patches.
✔ Lifespan: 10–15 years.

✔ Health problems: Hip dysplasia, ectropion, entropion.

The Eurasier was developed in the 1960s to bring back an extinct sledding breed of Russian Laika. Developed from the German Wolfspitz, Chow Chow, and Samoyed, this breed is rare in the United States.

Eurasiers are quiet, dignified, and reserved. They are one-person and one-family dogs and are aloof with strangers. They are highly independent like other Northern breeds, and are stubborn. They can be difficult to train. They make good guard dogs, although they are not noisy and therefore do not make good watchdogs. They can be dog-aggressive with a strong prey drive, so they should never be left alone with small pets.

Eurasiers must be socialized early. Although they are quite capable of withstanding the elements, they do not make good outdoor dogs. A Eurasier that does not have constant contact with his owner may become standoffish and aloof. Eurasiers need a moderate amount of exercise, comparing them to other Northern breeds, but may become destructive if bored.

Finnish Lapphund

✔ Registration available: UKC (Northern Breed).
✔ Size: Males: 18–20.5 inches (51–52 cm); females: 16–18.5 inches (41–47 cm); weight: 40–50 pounds (18–23 kg).
✔ Coat and colors: Double coat, sheds twice yearly; all colors permitted but one color must be predominate.
✔ Lifespan: 10–13 years.
✔ Health problems: Hip dysplasia.

The Finnish Lapphund is an ancient breed that comes from Norway, Sweden, and Finland, often referred to as Lapland. The Sami people of Lapland used spitz dogs to herd and hunt reindeer, their primary food source. Closely related to the Swedish Lapphund, which was also used for herding reindeer, the Finnish Lapphund is used for herding cattle and sheep and as a companion.

This dog has a high activity level. Like most shepherds, he is very loyal to his humans, but can be distrustful of other dogs. Very intelligent, he excels in obedience, agility, tracking, and of course, herding competitions. Not as stubborn as other Northern breeds, he still needs fair and consistent training. He might do well with other pets if properly raised with them. He can become a nuisance barker, if improperly trained.

Unless working, a Finnish Lapphund should stay with his family and most require the companionship of their owners. If bored, they can become destructive through chewing and digging.

Finnish Spitz

✔ Registration available: AKC (Non-Sporting) and UKC (Northern Breed).
✔ Size: Males: 17.5–20 inches (44–51 cm); females: 15.5–18 inches (39–46 cm); weight: 30–35 pounds (13.6–16 kg).
✔ Coat and colors: Double coat, sheds twice yearly; golden-red.
✔ Lifespan: 10–15 years.
✔ Health problems: Hip dysplasia and PRA.

Known as the Finnish Barking Bird Dog, the Finnish Spitz is an ancient breed that dates back several thousand years when the Finns inhabited Russia. As the Finns migrated, they took their hunting spitz dogs with them north to Finland. These dogs were kept isolated due

Chow Chow

Eurasian

to geography and remained pure for many centuries until modern times. By the 1880s the Finnish Spitz had been bred with many other dogs, threatening its extinction. Fortunately, a few purebreds were discovered and the breed was saved.

The Finnish Spitz is an active dog that is independent and stubborn. Highly intelligent, they are also highly vocal and can be prone to excessive barking. They make good watchdogs. They can be reserved with strangers, but are loving pets to their owners and families.

Although the Finnish Spitz is a hardy outdoor dog, he should stay with his family or he may not bond. These dogs are intelligent and become bored easily. They will focus their boredom on destructive activities such as chewing inappropriate objects, digging, and escaping.

German Spitz

✔ Registration available: None.
✔ Size: Giant: 16–18 inches (41–46 cm); weight: 35–40 pounds (16–18 kg); Standard: 12–15 inches (30–38 cm); weight: 25–35 pounds (11–16 kg); Toy: 8–11 inches (20–28 cm); weight: 15–25 pounds (7–11 kg).
✔ Coat and colors: Double coat, sheds often; solid colors include red, orange, cream, sable, black, gray, brown, and blue; brindle, parti-color, and black and tan are all acceptable.
✔ Lifespan: 10–15 years.
✔ Health problems: Joint problems, autoimmune diseases.

The German Spitz is a breed that appeared sometime during the Middle Ages, no doubt descended from indigenous spitz-type dogs. Not as popular as their close relatives, the Pomeranian, the German Spitz has been less overbred than many of its descendants. This breed has produced several other breeds including the German Wolfspitz, the Pomeranian, the American Eskimo, and the Keeshonden, to name a few.

The German Spitz is an active dog. Like many Northern Breeds, he is independent and stubborn, but can do well in obedience and agility if

Finnish Lapphund

Finnish Spitz

given consistent training. If poorly socialized and poorly trained, he can become aggressive, spoiled, and fearful of strangers. Normally reserved with strangers, he makes a good watchdog, but can become a nuisance barker.

German (Spitzen) do poorly as outdoor dogs. They are very inquisitive and demand a fair amount of attention from their owners. They can become destructive if bored.

Greenland Dog (see Canadian Inuit Dog)

Iceland Dog (Icelandic Sheepdog)
✔ Registration available: UKC (Northern Breed).
✔ Size: Males: 17–20 inches (43–51 cm); females: 15–18 inches (38–46 cm); weight: 30–40 pounds (14–18 kg).
✔ Coat and colors: Double coat, sheds twice yearly; two acceptable lengths—medium and long; any color, with one color predominant; white blaze and markings on chest, tip of tail, legs and toes acceptable.

✔ Lifespan: 10–15 years.
✔ Health problems: Hip dysplasia.

The Icelandic Sheepdog is an ancient breed, going back over 1,100 years. The Vikings brought this little dog to Iceland to herd their livestock. Currently an endangered species in Iceland, due to an outdated law that restricted dogs to farms, most Icelandic Sheepdog litters were destroyed. The law has recently been rescinded. The Icelandic Sheepdog is rare in the United States.

The Icelandic Sheepdog is a friendly, outgoing dog. Unlike other Northern breeds, he is friendly with all animals including cats, birds, and rabbits, but the owner of such animals should use caution when introducing these pets to any dog. The Icelandic Sheepdog is very people-oriented and will follow his owners around. He makes a good watchdog, but is not aggressive.

Icelandic Sheepdogs need a moderate amount of exercise. They are highly trainable and do well in obedience, agility, and other activities. Like most Northern breeds, they can become destructive if bored.

Jindo

✔ Registration available: UKC (Northern Breed).
✔ Size: Males: 19.5–21 inches (49.5–53 cm); weight: 35–45 pounds (16–20 kg); females: 18.5–20 inches (21.5–51 cm); weight: 30–40 pounds (14–18 kg).
✔ Coat and colors: Double coat, sheds twice yearly, medium length; off white with tan or brown highlights, fawn, gray, black and tan, and brindle; pure white is not allowed.
✔ Lifespan: 10–15 years.
✔ Health problems: Hip dysplasia.

The Jindo is an ancient breed from Korea. It is named for the island of Jindo, where in the 1200s, faced with the advance of the Mongols, the indigenous people's army withdrew. These soldiers took their fighting dogs with them and subsequently produced the purebred Jindo. Although the Korean government declared it a National Treasure in 1938, the Jindo on the mainland mixed with other indigenous dogs. The Jindo on the island remained pure. The Jindo is rare in the United States, but many exist in California and other areas where Korean immigrants settled.

Jindos are one-person or one-family dogs. They are loyal and gregarious to their owners, but suspicious of strangers, due to their guarding heritage. They are independent and can be very stubborn. They can be aggressive to other dogs. Because of their hunting heritage, they are not trustworthy around small animals.

Like all working dogs, Jindos take pleasure in performing a task. They are excellent hunters and will track game effortlessly. They make willing sledding and backpacking dogs. They can become destructive if bored.

Kai

✔ Registration available: UKC (Northern Breed).
✔ Size: Males: 18–22 inches (46–56 cm); weight: 35–55 pounds (16–25 kg); females: 17–20 inches (43–51 cm); weight: 25–45 pounds (11–20 kg).
✔ Coat and colors: Double coat, sheds twice yearly, medium length; any shade of brindle.
✔ Lifespan: 10–15 years.
✔ Health problems: Hip dysplasia.

The Kai is an ancient breed developed in Japan on the island on Honshu. It was developed primarily for hunting game, primarily deer and wild boar. The Japanese call the Kai the Tora Dog both for his legendary courage and toughness and for the brindle or striped pattern of his coat color. This breed was not recognized until 1934 in Japan.

Once thought to be too primitive for a good pet, the Kai's personality is one of loyalty and gentleness. He gets along well with humans and other pets, although the owner should always take precautions when introducing cats or other pets. He makes a good watchdog and guard dog. He is moderately active and needs daily exercise.

Although Kais can live outdoors, they need to stay with their family to bond and socialize. Like all working dogs, they take pleasure in performing a task. They can become destructive if bored.

Karelian Bear Dog (Karelian Bear Laika)

✔ Registration available: UKC (Northern Breed).
✔ Size: Males: 21.25–23.5 inches (55–60 cm); weight: 45–60 pounds (20–27 kg); females: 19.25–21.25 inches (49–54 cm); weight: 40–55 pounds (18–25 kg).
✔ Coat and colors: Double coat, sheds twice yearly, medium length; black and white; black to

white ratio preferred is 7:3, but 8:2, 6:4, 9:1, and 5:5 is acceptable.

✔ Lifespan: 10–13 years.

✔ Health problems: Hip dysplasia.

The Karelian Bear Dog and its close relative, the Karelian Bear Laika, came from ancient spitz stock developed by the indigenous people of the Karelian Forests in Finland. These dogs were used at the turn of the nineteenth century to hunt bear, wolf, lynx, deer, and birds. Although the Finish Kennel Club recognized the breed when registrations exceeded 100, it is an ancient breed with roots going back as far as 900 A.D. with the Komi people from Russia. In 1947 the Soviets ordained that Karelian Bear Dogs were not Laika, and the Karelian Bear Laika or Russo-European Laika were recognized by the Soviets as Karelian Bear Laika or Dogs. Slightly bigger than the Karelian Bear Dog, these dogs are obviously related to their Finnish counterparts.

Karelian Bear Dogs are strong, agile hunters. They are often dog-aggressive and aggressive toward other animals. They are independent and stubborn and need much socialization and training. Very active dogs, they are not satisfied to be kept strictly as pets. They are very loyal to their family and mistrustful of strangers. One unusual characteristic is that they can be born with a natural bobbed tail.

Like all working dogs, they take pleasure in performing tasks. They are excellent hunters and will track game and then hold it. They make willing sledding and backpacking dogs. They can become destructive if bored.

Keeshond

✔ Registration available: AKC (Non-sporting) and UKC (Northern Breed).

✔ Size: Males: 17–19 inches (43–48 cm); weight: 35–45 pounds (16–20 kg); females: 16–18 inches (41–46 cm); weight: 30–40 pounds (14–18 kg).

✔ Coat and colors: Double coat, sheds frequently, long in length; wolf gray with a light gray or cream undercoat; has a mask or "spectacles" around the eyes.

✔ Lifespan: 10–15 years.

✔ Health problems: Hip dysplasia, skin conditions.

The Keeshond, pronounced KAZE-hund, is an ancient breed from Holland that served as a barge dog and companion. Made popular by the Patriot, Kees de Gyselaer, in the late 1700s, the medium-sized dog with the spectacles was the constant companion of Kees, earning the breed its name.

The Keeshond is an excellent companion dog with a thick coat, capable of withstanding deep cold. He is cheerful and always eager to please. Less independent than his Northern breed cousin, Keeshonden require companionship and consistent training. They are very sensitive dogs that do not do well with harsh training. They are moderately active, but can thrive in an urban environment.

One interesting trait is that a Keeshond will "smile," that is, bare his teeth in a sneer or smile when happy or greeting people. This should never be interpreted as aggression. Keeshonden are also known to "bluster," that is, become very excited and noisy. They can be snappy if spoiled or improperly trained. They can also become yappy and may bark incessantly. They are good around cats and other dogs, if raised with them.

Lapponian Herder

✔ Registration available: UKC (Northern Breed).

✔ Size: Males: 17–19 inches (43–48 cm); weight: 35–45 pounds (16–20 kg); females:

German Spitz

Icelandic Sheepdog

16–18 inches (41–46 cm); weight: 30–40 pounds (14–18 kg).

✔ Coat and colors: Double coat, sheds frequently, short to medium in length; all colors are accepted, including solid white; common colors include black and tan, brown and tan, and black with brown or gray markings.

✔ Lifespan: 10–15 years.

✔ Health problems: Hip dysplasia, PRA.

German Spitz (wolfspitz)

The Lapponian Herder is an ancient breed from Norway, Sweden, and Finland, often referred to as Lapland. This is one of many ancient breeds that the Sami people of Lapland used to herd and hunt reindeer, their primary food source.

Unlike the Border Collie that uses its eyes to control sheep, the Lapponian Herder barks to control the reindeer and chases them to herd them into a tight group. This dog has a high activity level, enabling him to trot for miles for hours on end. Built for movement and speed, the Lapponian Herder is a true working dog.

Like most shepherds, he is very loyal to his humans, but can be distrustful of other dogs. Very intelligent, he excels in obedience, agility, tracking, and of course, herding competitions. A seemingly tireless worker, he is willing to take on any new task for his owner. Not as stubborn as other Northern breeds, he still needs fair and consistent training. If bored, he can become destructive through chewing and digging. He might do well with other pets if

Jindo

Karelian Bear Dog

Keeshonden

Norwegian Puffin Dog (Lundehunde)

properly raised with them. He can become a nuisance barker, if improperly trained.

Lundehunde (Norwegian Lundehund, Norwegian Puffin Dog)

✔ Registration available: UKC (Northern Breed).

✔ Size: Males: 13.75–15 inches (35–38 cm); weight: 15.5 pounds (7 kg); females: 12.5–13.75 inches (31.7–35 cm); weight: 13.25 pounds (6 kg).
✔ Coat and colors: Double coat, sheds twice yearly, medium in length; reddish-brown to fallow, black, gray and white; may have white markings.

✔ Lifespan: 10–15 years.

✔ Health problems: Hip dysplasia, cryp-torchidism, PRA.

The Norwegian Puffin Dog is an ancient breed, perhaps going back over 5,000 years or more. This breed has unusual characteristics not found in other dogs, such as six toes (not double dewclaws), a flexible, double-jointed neck that can bend backward until the nose touches the spine, flexible shoulders and forelegs, and an extra fold across the ear cartilage that enables the dog to fold the ears down. All of these unusual traits appear to help the Lundehund in its original purpose—hunting puffins (birds) along the craggy rocks and cliffs on Norwegian islands.

This breed is a companion dog now. Puffin Dogs are generally nonaggressive and get along with most dogs and even cats. Due to their history, they should not be kept with birds, which they consider prey. They are not as stubborn and dominance-oriented as other Northern breeds, but still need fair and consistent training. They will cache food and enjoy carrying around items.

While Puffin Dogs do well outdoors, they should never be considered outdoor-only dogs. They are very sensitive and need socialization and exposure to new situations to avoid becoming shy. Like most Northern breeds, they become destructive if bored.

Norwegian Buhund

✔ Registration available: UKC (Northern Breed).

✔ Size: Males: 16–17 inches (41–43 cm); weight: 30–40 pounds (13.6–18 kg); females: 15–16 inches (38–40.6 cm); weight: 25–35 pounds (11–16 kg).

✔ Coat and colors: Double coat, sheds twice yearly, medium in length; wheaten with black markings or black with white markings.

✔ Lifespan: 10–15 years.

✔ Health problems: Hip dysplasia, PRA.

The Norwegian Buhund is a smaller spitz-derived dog that originally was used for herding livestock. His ancestry goes back to ancient times when he helped shepherds tend their flocks. More trainable and family-oriented than other breeds, he is moderately active for a Northern breed and makes a good pet, provided he is given something to do. He can become destructive if bored.

Fast and intelligent, the Norwegian Buhund does well in obedience and agility. He makes an excellent watchdog but may become a nuisance barker. Some Norwegian Buhunds may be suspicious of strangers. Due to his herding heritage, he may nip or "herd" other animals or people. Like most shepherds, he is loyal to his family.

Norwegian Buhunds make poor outside dogs because of the need to be with their humans. They can adapt to cats and other small animals provided they are properly introduced.

Norwegian Elkhound

✔ Registration available: AKC (Hound) and UKC (Northern Breed).

✔ Size: Males: 20.5 inches (52 cm); weight: 55 pounds (25 kg); females: 19.5 inches (49 cm); weight: 48 pounds (22 kg).

✔ Coat and colors: Double coat, sheds often, medium in length; gray with black markings and a silver undercoat.

✔ Lifespan: 10–15 years.

✔ Health problems: Hip dysplasia, PRA.

The Norwegian Elkhound dates back to at least 5000 B.C., where a loyal Elkhound was entombed beside his Viking master. The Elkhound was used in Norway to hunt bear and moose (the word "elk" actually refers to moose, not the North American elk.) Obviously derived from an ancient spitz line, the Elkhound's primary purpose is as a hunting partner.

This adaptable breed makes a good pet if given enough outdoor exercise. He enjoys backpacking, agility, and flyball. Most are friendly with strangers, but some can be reserved. He can be stubborn and may have dominance issues, if not trained in a fair, consistent manner. Unless raised with other pets, an Elkhound will consider them prey. Some Elkhounds are dog-aggressive and must be socialized young with other dogs. They make good watchdogs, but can become nuisance barkers.

Norwegian Elkhounds make poor outside dogs due to their independent natures. They are intelligent and become bored easily. Elkhounds will focus their boredom on destructive chewing, digging, and escaping.

Pomeranian

✔ Registration available: AKC (Toy) and UKC (Northern Breed).
✔ Size: 6–7 inches (15–18 cm); weight: 3–7 pounds (1.4–3 kg).
✔ Coat and colors: Double coat, sheds often; solid colors include red, orange, cream, sable, black, brown, and blue; brindle, parti-color, and black and tan are all acceptable.
✔ Lifespan: 10–15 years.
✔ Health problems: Joint problems, autoimmune diseases, eye infections, heart problems.

The Pomeranian is a breed descended from German spitz lines in Pomerania, Germany. These lines originated from Icelandic sled dogs, bred down for size. The Pomeranian was relatively unknown until Queen Victoria acquired one in 1888 and bolstered the breed's popularity. The Pomeranian still resembles its predecessor, the German Spitz, but is smaller than the toy German Spitz variety.

The Pomeranian is an active dog for a toy breed. Like many Northern breeds, he is independent and stubborn, but can do well in obedience and agility if given consistent training. If poorly socialized and poorly trained, he can become aggressive, spoiled, and fearful of strangers. Normally reserved with strangers, he makes a good watchdog, but can become a nuisance barker.

Pomeranians do poorly as outdoor dogs. They are very inquisitive and demand a fair amount of attention from their owners. They can become destructive if bored.

Russo-European Laika (see Karelian Bear Dog)

Samoyed

✔ Registration available: AKC (Working) and UKC (Northern Breed).
✔ Size: Males: 21–23.5 inches (53–59.6 cm); weight: 55–70 pounds (25–32 kg); females: 19–21 inches (48–53 cm); weight: 45–55 pounds (20–25 kg).
✔ Coat and colors: Double coat, sheds twice yearly; white, biscuit, or cream.
✔ Lifespan: 10–15 years.
✔ Health problems: Hip dysplasia, elbow dysplasia, low thyroid, zinc dermatitis, CPRA, PRA.

The Samoyed is an ancient breed that came from Samoyed peoples in Siberia. These nomadic hunters used the Samoyed to herd reindeer and to pull sleds. Believed to have been derived from an ancient line, without mixing wolf or other dog breeds, the Samoyed

Norwegian Buhund

Norwegian Elkhound

Pomeranian

Samoyed

peoples created an all-around dog capable of many tasks. Samoyeds have been used on many famous polar expeditions.

The Samoyed is a friendly, outgoing dog. He should never be aggressive toward people or other dogs. He makes a good watchdog, but may become a nuisance barker. Unless raised with other pets, Samoyeds consider them prey. Samoyeds are also very pack-oriented and may challenge their owners for dominance. They are stubborn and sometimes difficult to train, but once the owner has the dog's respect, can perform admirably in obedience, agility, herding, and other competitions.

Shiba Inu

Siberian Husky

Samoyeds can live either indoors or outdoors, if they receive enough attention and exercise, but prefer to live with their owners. These dogs are intelligent and become easily bored. They will focus their boredom on destructive activities such as chewing inappropriate objects, digging, and escaping. These dogs excel in backpacking and sledding.

Shiba Inu
✔ Registration available: AKC (Non-Sporting) and UKC (Northern Breed).
✔ Size: males: 14.5–16.5 inches (37–42 cm); weight: 23 pounds (10 kg); females: 13.5–15.5 inches (34–39 cm); weight: 17 pounds (7.7 kg).
✔ Coat and colors: Double coat, medium length, sheds often; red, black, and sesame.
✔ Lifespan: 10–15 years.
✔ Health problems: Luxating patella, autoimmune diseases, eye defects, heart problems.

The Shiba is an ancient breed; its ancestors accompanied its owners into Japan some 7,000 years ago. These dogs mixed with the indigenous dogs, producing a small dog, capable of hunting both small and large game. Originally used to hunt small game and birds, it quickly became a popular pet as well as an able hunter. These dogs were declared a Natural Monument in 1937 along with the Akita and Ainu.

The Shiba Inu is an independent and active breed. Like his larger cousin, the Akita, he can be protective and dog-aggressive. Shibas have an extremely strong prey drive and may kill small animals such as cats unless raised with them as puppies.

Shiba Inus do not do well as outside dogs. They need to be with their owners to bond. They are intelligent and become bored easily. They will focus their boredom on destructive activities such as chewing inappropriate objects and digging. They are active dogs and require daily exercise.

Siberian Husky
✔ Registration available: AKC (Working) and UKC (Northern Breed).

✔ Size: males: 21–23.5 inches (53–59.6 cm); weight: 45–60 pounds (20–27 kg); females: 20–22 inches (51–56 cm); weight: 35–50 pounds (16–23 kg).

✔ Coat and colors: Double coat, sheds twice yearly; all colors acceptable.

✔ Lifespan: 10–15 years.

✔ Health problems: Hip dysplasia, elbow dysplasia, low thyroid, zinc dermatitis, CPRA, PRA.

The Siberian Husky is an ancient breed that came from the Chukchi tribe that lived in northeastern Asia. These nomadic hunters required a medium-sized dog capable of pulling light loads over great distances. William Goosak, a Russian fur trader, first brought Siberians to Alaska to race in the famous All-Alaskan Sweepstakes in Nome.

The Siberian Husky is a friendly, outgoing dog. He should never be aggressive toward people or other dogs. He makes a poor watchdog and guard dog. This is an independent breed, and does not follow his owner around. Unless raised with other pets, Siberian Huskies consider them prey. Siberian Huskies are also very pack-oriented and may challenge their owners for dominance.

Siberian Huskies can live either indoors or outdoors, if they receive enough attention and exercise. They are intelligent and become bored easily. Siberians will focus their boredom on destructive activities such as chewing inappropriate objects, digging, and escaping. They excel in backpacking and sledding.

Swedish Lapphund

✔ Registration available: UKC (Northern Breed).

✔ Size: Males: 18–20.5 inches (15–52 cm); females: 16–18.5 inches (41–47 cm); weight: 40–50 pounds (18–23 kg).

✔ Coat and colors: Double coat, sheds twice yearly; black.

✔ Lifespan: 10–15 years.

✔ Health problems: Hip dysplasia, PRA.

The Swedish Lapphund is an ancient breed that comes from Norway, Sweden, and Finland, often referred to as Lapland. The Sami people of Lapland used spitz dogs to herd and hunt reindeer, their primary food source. Closely related to the Finnish Lapphund, which was also used for herding reindeer, the Swedish Lapphund is used for herding and as a companion. The Swedish Lapphund and the Finnish Lapphund are, in essence, the same breed, with superficial differences.

The Swedish Lapphund is a companion animal. This dog has a high activity level and is still capable of herding. Like most shepherds, he is very loyal to his humans, but can be distrustful of other dogs. Very intelligent, he excels in obedience, agility, tracking, and of course, herding competitions. He still needs fair and consistent training. He might do well with other pets, if properly raised with them. He can become a nuisance barker, if improperly trained.

A Swedish Lapphund should not be an outdoor-only dog. Most Swedish Lapphunds require their owners companionship. If bored, they can become destructive through chewing and digging.

Thai Ridgeback

✔ Registration available: UKC (Northern Breed).

✔ Size: Males: 19–24 inches (48–61 cm); females: 23–25 inches (58–63.5 cm); weight: 37–53 pounds (17–24 kg).

✔ Coat and colors: Double coat—some are now single coat—short, sheds frequently; black, red, fawn, beige, blue, brindle, and white.

✔ Lifespan: 10–13 years.

✔ Health problems: Hip dysplasia, PRA, ectropion, entropion.

The Thai Ridgeback is a pariah dog that has existed for at least 5,000 years. Although short coated and "houndy," national and international breed clubs have identified this breed as a Spitz. The older type has a thin undercoat, although certain lines may no longer have undercoats. Originally, the Thai Ridgeback was bred from the indigenous dogs (Mah Thai) for guarding and hunting. Some Thai Ridgeback fanciers suggest that the Chinese Shar-pei may have come from the Thai Ridgeback.

Thai Ridgebacks are affectionate with their own families, but are reserved with strangers. They can be independent like other Northern breeds and are stubborn. They can be difficult to train. They make good guard dogs and good watchdogs. They can be dog-aggressive and have a strong prey drive, so they should never be left alone with small pets such as cats. Some breeders and trainers are training Thai Ridgebacks for attack work, so some lines will be more aggressive than others.

Due to their thin coats, they do not make good outdoor dogs. Thai Ridgebacks require socialization or may become standoffish and aloof. They are active dogs and need a moderate amount of exercise, comparing them to other Northern breeds. They may become destructive if bored.

West Siberian Laika

✔ Registration available: UKC (Northern Breed).

✔ Size: 20–25 inches (51–63.5 cm); weight: 40–55 pounds (18–25 kg).

✔ Coat and colors: Double coat, short to medium, sheds twice yearly; white, red, gray, gray and white, black and white.

✔ Lifespan: 10–15 years.

✔ Health problems: Hip dysplasia.

The West Siberian Laika originated from indigenous dogs in Ural and West Siberia, particularly dogs owned by the Zyryan, Mansi, and Hanty peoples. Like his counterpart, the East Siberian Laika, he was used to hunt big game and pull sleds in Siberia, although his main purpose was as a hunting dog. Unlike the ESL, this breed is older, although it's recognition as a breed was not established until the 1930s when the Soviet government officially recognized it as a breed.

Although wolflike in appearance, this Laika is trainable when compared to other Northern Breeds. WSL excel in obedience, hunting, and agility competitions. Independent and stubborn, he requires consistent training. Unless raised with other pets, WSL consider them prey.

WSL are capable of staying outdoors, but should stay with their families for proper socialization. These dogs are intelligent and become bored easily. They will focus their boredom on destructive activities such as chewing inappropriate objects, digging, and escaping.

CHOOSING A NORTHERN BREED

No doubt, a Northern breed's handsome looks have charmed you, but do you know everything about the particular breed? Do you want a watchdog or a guard? Many Northern breeds make poor watchdogs and guard dogs and will welcome anyone into your home, friend or foe. Do you want a trainable dog, one that walks nicely on leash and obeys commands readily? Again, many Northern breeds are independent and pull on the leash as though they were running the Iditarod. Many are untrustworthy off leash because of their overwhelming desire to run. Consider your needs before you buy!

What to Consider Before You Choose

Male or Female?

In most Northern breeds, there is a marked difference between males and females; however, the dog's overall personality overrides any generalities. Males tend to be more dominance-oriented and more conscious of pack hierarchy. Females may or may not be dominance-oriented; if they are, they tend to be very assertive when it comes to their "Alpha-

No doubt, a Northern breed's handsome looks have charmed you, but do you know everything about the particular breed? These are Finnish Spitzen.

ness" in the pack. Some males tend to be cuddlers, that is, very attached to their humans. Females may be loving, but tend to be more "businesslike"—not necessarily aloof, but not willing to spend long hours being petted.

Puppy or Adult?

Many people prefer to purchase a puppy rather than an adult dog. Puppies are cuter, certainly, and have not had the chance to learn bad habits. Also, it generally takes less time for a puppy to bond with a new owner than an adult dog. However, puppies are time consuming. They are not housebroken, they are often destructive chewers, and they require extensive training. You cannot expect a puppy to "hold it" for eight hours or more a day. Puppies cry during the first few nights, so you

TIP

Nordic Dog Personalities

Some Nordic dog personalities are reserved to aloof to shy. This will occur more often in large kennels where the dog may not have had the chance to bond with people. However, if Yukon is naturally shy or aloof, he will display those tendencies to a lesser degree with proper socialization.

should not expect to get much sleep. If you are looking for a conformation or working dog, a puppy is a definite risk. A promising puppy may not turn into the show or working prospect you intended. Finally, if no one is at home during the day to train, socialize, and watch over the puppy, consider purchasing or adopting an adult dog.

Wolf Hybrids

Some people find it fashionable to own a wolf or wolf hybrid, thinking that what they will get is a wolfy-looking dog. Nothing could be further from the truth!

Imagine all the negative traits of the Northern breeds amplified and add complete unpredictability. That is a wolf or wolf-hybrid. If you find a sweet, even-tempered hybrid, consider yourself lucky—and consider how many other dogs came into this world and were put down for temperament. Can you make a wolf or wolf-hybrid work out? Maybe, if you do not expect a wild animal to behave like a pet. If you are still determined to own a wolf hybrid, contact a trained professional or wolf sanctu-

ary to teach you how to live with a wolf or wolf hybrid cross.

Where to Find a Northern Breed Puppy

Puppies are adorable and Northern breeds are no exception, but puppies should not be bought on impulse, because most Northern breeds live an average of 10 to 15 years. Always purchase a dog from a reputable breeder. When you purchase a puppy or an adult dog from a reputable breeder, that breeder has done extensive testing to help ensure that the puppy has a sound temperament and is free from genetic diseases. All reputable breeders offer a health guarantee and will take the puppy back anytime during its life, whether it is a six-month-old puppy or a six-year-old dog.

CHECKLIST

✔ A wolf is a wild animal bereft of the thousands of years of domestication necessary to make a dog.

✔ A wolf hybrid is neither wolf nor dog, but somewhere in-between. It has the instinct and the wildness of the wolf, with the conflicting messages from dog genetics, making it highly unpredictable.

✔ Some wolf hybrids are very sweet natured until there is some trigger that brings out the wildness. It may be something as simple as putting down a food bowl or walking by. Then the owner is shocked by the dog's aggressive display.

CHECKLIST

Is a Northern Breed Right for You?

✔ Are you able to give your Northern breed daily attention?

✔ Are you able to brush your Northern breed frequently? Some require daily brushings.

✔ Can you afford the cost of dog ownership? The cost of a dog does not end at its purchase price. Northern breeds require premium dog food, veterinary care (both routine and emergency), supplies, and other expenses generally associated with owning a dog.

✔ Are you willing to spend 10 to 15 years caring for this dog? Most Northern breeds live on an average of 10 to 15 years, although some breeds may have an 8- to 12-year life span, and others have a 15- to 20-year life span.

✔ Are you willing to deal with dog hair? Most Northern breeds shed or "blow coat" twice a year, where the fur literally comes out by the handful. If you are a fastidious person, or if someone in your household is allergic to dogs, then a Northern breed is not for you.

✔ Are you able to exercise your Northern breed every day? Going for a walk does not constitute exercise for most of these dogs, particularly the sledding breeds. Backpacking, skijoring, sledding, agility, and other physical activities are an absolute must for these dogs or they will become bored and restless. Two days of the week should be dedicated toward some activity, with regular exercise such as walks on the other days.

✔ Are you willing to enroll your Northern breed in obedience training classes? Obedience training is a *must* for a pet Northern breed.

✔ Are you willing to put up with destructive tendencies? Many Northern breeds dig trenches better than the Army Corp of Engineers, chew wood faster than a beaver, and may destroy "indestructible" items. Puppies must be housebroken and even adult dogs may have an occasional accident.

✔ Does everyone in the household want a Northern breed? All family members must agree to the dog before bringing one home.

How to Find a Reputable Breeder

Too often, the buyer is more concerned over whether the breeder is "a nice person." "Nice people" run puppy mills, dump puppies into animal shelters, and breed dysplastic dogs. A puppy mill owner and a backyard breeder are going to be pleasant, because they want your business. Reputable breeders may not seem "nice" because they ask tough questions. They ask tough questions because they care where they sells their Northern breed puppies. They will often turn down ready buyers in order to find the best homes for them. They will ask questions about you, your family, and your home that may seem intrusive, but they are a sign that the breeder really cares about the new home their Northern breed puppies are going to.

You should also be asking questions concerning the puppies and their parents. Do the parents have working titles, show titles, or obedience titles? What are the dogs' merits that make them worthwhile to breed? Have the breeders screened for genetic diseases?

Breeder Contracts

Ask the breeder for the contract *before* seeing the puppies. The contract should clearly stipulate the terms of the sale. Should you read the contract and not understand it, have an attorney look it over.

The contract should have a guarantee that the puppy or dog is free from genetic diseases and is healthy. Most breeders require the owner to take the puppy to the veterinarian between 24 to 72 hours after purchase to confirm the puppy's health. Guarantees for hip dysplasia and eye problems may have a time limit of two to five years and may have certain exclusions. The breeder will usually refund all or part of the puppy's purchase price or provide a suitable replacement. The contract should also have what is called "First Right of

Refusal." This means that the owner must first contact the breeder before selling or giving away the dog. All reputable breeders will take back the dog they sold to prevent them from going to a backyard breeder, puppy mill, animal shelter or an unsuitable home.

The contract will also require that you will take adequate care of your Northern breed. You may be required to have a fenced-in yard or kennel and that you will not allow your Nordic dog to roam. If the puppy is sold as a pet, you may have to spay or neuter it before it reaches six months of age. If the puppy is show quality, you may be required to obtain OFA and CERF certification before breeding it.

The contract should not limit your ownership on the puppy. You should never be forced into co-ownership, especially if you are paying a fair purchase price. You should not be required to breed your puppy nor to owe a puppy from some future litter back to the breeder. This is unfair to you because you

Adult Northern breeds may come from anywhere—even from retired sled dogs. These are Alaskan Huskies.

Never buy a puppy on impulse. Northern breeds are a 10–15 year commitment. These are Siberian Husky puppies.

shouldn't have to provide stock to this breeder, especially if you just want a pet. Likewise, the guarantees should not have clauses where they will not be honored unless certain unusual conditions are fulfilled. Any conditions on the guarantees should be reasonable and not include bizarre homemade diets or limiting the amount of sensible exercise.

Choosing an Adult Northern Breed

Choosing an adult Northern Breed is different from choosing a puppy. A puppy is full of unknowns and surprises as it grows, whereas the adult is a known quantity. However, you should choose an adult with a stable personality.

The adult Northern breed should be outgoing and friendly. Avoid any timid or aggressive dogs. If the Nordic dog knows commands, walk

him on a leash and practice the commands. Don't be surprised if he pulls on a leash—this is very common. Offer him a treat whenever he performs the command correctly.

Call the dog to you and clap your hands. He should show interest at the sound of a friendly voice, but he may show some independence and may not come immediately or may not come at all without food to lure him. Watch for any unusual behavior, if the Nordic dog behaves differently than you expected, you may have to look elsewhere.

Ask the breeder or rescue staff if this dog is housebroken, crate-trained, and obedience-trained. Find out what bad habits this Nordic dog has, if any. Ask her why the dog is available. If the dog is a returned animal, ask the breeder or rescue staff why it was returned. Ask for the name and phone number of the former owners and talk with them, if this is

CHECKLIST

Questions You Should Ask a Breeder

✔ Does the breeder have only one or two breeds that she breeds? Reputable breeders focus on one or two breeds to improve the standard.

✔ Does the breeder belong to a national or local breed club?

✔ Do the puppies' parents have conformation, obedience, working, or agility titles? If you are looking to purchase a working dog, ask what races the parents have run and what position in the team they ran.

✔ How did the breeder choose the stud dog? Was it a dog she owned or did she search for the right dog to breed to her own female? The female shouldn't have been bred to what was available, but rather, to a dog that would improve the conformation and bloodline of the stock.

✔ Can the breeder provide photographs and information concerning the parents, grandparents, great-grandparents, uncles, aunts, and cousins of the puppies? If she cannot tell you about these dogs, then how is she able to breed a quality Northern breed?

✔ Is there OFA and CERF certification on both parents? OFA certification comes from the Orthopedic Foundation for Animals. The hips should be at least a Good rating, preferably Excellent. CERF certification comes from the Canine Eye Registry Foundation. The rating is either Passed or Failed. Ask to see the *original* certificates if the breeder has both parents. If the breeder has only the female, ask to see her original certificate and a photocopy from the male's owners.

✔ How old are the puppies' parents? Neither parent should be bred before two years old. They cannot have their OFA certification until then.

✔ Why did the breeder breed these two dogs? The answer should be to produce puppies to improve the breed. Often, the breeder will keep one or two puppies to see if they will become show or working prospects, but occasionally breeders will not keep a puppy because it did not turn out as they thought it would. Never buy a puppy from someone who is breeding dogs to make a profit. Don't buy a puppy from someone who wanted a dog just like his or her pet. The breeder should be striving to improve the breed, not breed pet-quality puppies.

✔ Ask the breeder for a contract, which is your bill of sale. The AKC or UKC papers are not a bill of sale. If the breeder does not have a contract, look elsewhere. She should stipulate that she will take the dog back under any conditions. The breeder should also guarantee that the puppy is free from illnesses, parasites, and hereditary defects. She will stipulate that you must adequately care for the puppy and will require that you must never allow your Nordic dog to run at large. The contract should not have stud rights or requirements for breeding unless this is something you've agreed on prior to seeing the contract. The guarantee should not have a caveat such as strange diets or extreme limitation of exercise.

✔ Ask for registration papers. If you purchase a puppy that the American Kennel Club (AKC) or the United Kennel Club (UKC) recognizes as purebred, the breeder should furnish puppy registration papers as proof that your puppy is purebred. These registration papers do not mean that your Nordic puppy is somehow more valuable than anyone else's, nor is it a guarantee of quality. It is a guarantee that the puppy is purebred and has a purebred pedigree.

✔ Reputable breeders will not press you to buy a puppy. They will first try to educate you as to what it means to own a Northern breed, then they will tell you about the good points and the shortcomings of the breed. They may ask for references.

✔ How long has the breeder been involved with Northern breeds? Backyard breeders are usually new at breeding Northern Breeds. Occasionally, this is a reputable breeder's first litter, but she is also very involved in showings.

✔ When were the puppies wormed and vaccinated? A reputable breeder will either worm the puppies or have a veterinarian perform a fecal analysis on the puppies to determine if worms are present. Puppies should have received their first vaccinations at five to six weeks of age.

✔ When is the earliest the breeder will allow you to take a puppy? The youngest a Northern Breed puppy should leave its mother is eight weeks old—no exceptions.

✔ What items will the breeder provide when you are ready to take your Northern breed home? The breeder should provide information on raising and training a Northern breed, the puppy contract, the AKC papers, copies of the parents' OFA and CERF certification, a sample of the food the puppy has been receiving, a record of vaccinations and worming, a vaccination schedule, a pedigree, and any other information the breeder thinks might be useful to a new owner. Some breeders may include a toy to help ease the puppy into its new home.

✔ Ask for references. The breeder should be able to provide you with names and phone numbers of other members of the national or local club and people who have bought puppies who will gladly vouch for this breeder.

practical. Ask them why they returned the dog. They may be candid and tell you about the dog you are considering.

Shelters and Rescues

Sadly, every year thousands of purebred and mixed Northern breeds are dumped into shelters or appear in rescues. People purchase or adopt these dogs, ignorant of their heritage as working dogs. These people are unwilling to invest the time necessary to work toward training, socializing, and exercising them.

Because of the unique nature of the Northern breeds and their intense desire to work and belong in a pack, many of these dogs have exhibited their frustration in the forms of destructive behavior. Other situations include the death of the owner, a child that has allergies, or moving to an apartment where dogs are not allowed.

Can you find the perfect Northern breed for you at the shelter? If you are patient and willing to provide extra training and socialization, you may find a dog to be your lifelong companion.

Even the littlest Pomeranian is descended from sled dogs.

A normal reaction to being held and cuddled might be a little apprehension followed by cheerful acceptance. The model is an American Eskimo puppy.

Shiba Inu. The name means "little dog" in Japanese.

A beautiful Siberian Husky.

How can you choose between them all? If you have found a reputable breeder, he or she may have already selected your companion based on personality. This recommendation may be determined by whether you intend your Northern Breed to be a working, show, or companion dog. He or she has had time to observe the puppies' personalities.

✔ When you are about to select a puppy, first observe the puppies. You don't want a shy or timid puppy because it will most likely be shy or timid the rest of its life. You don't want an overly independent and stubborn puppy because it will be headstrong and difficult to train and won't listen to your commands. You want a puppy that is interested in you. Often, the puppy that comes to you first may be too dominant, so don't be fooled into thinking that it chose you. Instead, watch how the puppies interact; that it will give you a good clue as to their personalities.

✔ With the breeder's permission, separate each puppy you are considering from the litter and observe its reactions as you pet and cuddle it. At this point, the dam may become nervous or overly protective. The breeder may have to separate her from puppies in order for you to perform your tests. Ask the breeder to do so if he or she does not.

✔ A normal reaction to being held and cuddled individually might be a little apprehension followed by cheerful acceptance. Gently place the puppy on its back and hold it there. It may struggle or yip for a few moments and then quiet down as you rub its tummy. If the puppy reacts aggressively by either trying to nip or struggling violently, let it go. This puppy is very dominant and may be difficult for you to train. Likewise, if the puppy cries and submissively urinates, the puppy is *too* submissive and timid. You should not pick either of those puppies.

✔ Test your puppy by rolling a ball or tossing a toy. It should go after it eagerly and play, not shy submissively away from it or ignore it. Puppies have short attention spans so you may have to throw it a few times before you get the puppy's attention. Clap your hands and call to the puppies. They should come over to investigate.

✔ Look at all the puppies. Are they clean, bright-eyed, and well cared-for? Are they alert and attentive? You may have awakened them from a nap, but they should still respond well to you. If the puppies act lethargic or cry piteously, you should maybe consider

Puppies in a well-bred litter should all show some physical consistency.

PUPPY FROM THE LITTER

When visiting a breeder in your search for a puppy, observe how the puppies react to one another and to their mother. Also watch her behavior with the puppies. It will tell you a lot about the puppy you are considering.

It is normal for a puppy to be a little apprehensive when being held on its back to be cuddled. It won't take long for the puppy to calm down and enjoy the attention.

another litter. Anything unusual, such as distended bellies might indicate a problem.
✔ One puppy will no doubt be your favorite. Pick it up and snap your fingers behind its

head. It should turn and look, or at least respond. Wave a toy in front of its face and see if the puppy will try to grab it. These tests may help identify a deaf or blind puppy.

BRINGING YOUR NEW DOG HOME

For the first few weeks, you may wish to confine Yukon to one or two rooms to limit his destructiveness. Baby gates are a good deterrent— for a while. Most Northern breeds figure out baby gates quickly and learn to climb or jump them. If Yukon is large enough, he may actually walk straight through the gate and knock it down, so it is better that you prepare by dog-proofing your home.

Puppy and Dog-proofing Your Home

Living Room
✔ Remove all knickknacks from tables that Tasha can reach either from her normal height or by standing on her hind legs.
✔ Hide all electrical cords behind furniture and be certain that Yukon cannot slip behind the furniture to reach them.
✔ Put all shoes, clothing, and any interesting item—to the dog—behind closed doors.
✔ Put coins and small metal objects in a jar, away from Yukon. Pennies, especially newer ones, are mostly zinc and may give him "penny poisoning." Nails, tacks, needles, and other sharp items can severely injure your dog or puppy.

Northern breeds have a tendency to roam, so always keep your Northern breed in a fenced back yard. A Norwegian Buhund takes a peek over the fence.

✔ Move household plants out of reach of the dog; many are poisonous.

Kitchen
✔ Do not leave food out on the counter—ever.
✔ Install baby latches on cabinets under counters. Install a baby latch—usually a hook and loop strap, such as Velcro—on the refrigerator.
✔ Put trash containers behind a closed door in the pantry, garage, or under a cabinet where Tasha cannot access it. Trash can contain rotten food and other poisonous items that can make Tasha very sick.

Bathroom/ Laundry Room
✔ Keep all medicines in a medicine cabinet away from Yukon. Keep toothpaste, mouthwash, and other enticing items away from inquisitive noses.

Note: To avoid using the impersonal "it," this book refers to individual dogs as Yukon and Tasha.

✔ Laundry should stay in a laundry hamper away from Tasha.

✔ Keep cleaning materials that are poisonous away from your Northern breed.

Fence, Kennel, or Tied-out?

Fences: Anyone who owns a Northern breed *must* have a fenced-in backyard or kennel run. If you own a medium to large Northern breed, you should have a minimum of a 6-foot-tall (1.8 cm) fence that is climb-proof, dig-proof, and jump-proof. Owners of smaller dogs, such as Pomeranians and Alaskan Klee Kai may be able to get by with no fenced yard, or outdoor kennel and frequent walks, but this is a serious commitment.

Many Northern breed owners live in suburban and rural settings, believing that it is best to let Yukon run free to get his exercise. Once turned loose, Nordics quickly become nuisances. They frequently join packs of other semiferal dogs. They will raid garbage cans, chase game and

---

TIP

The Car Ride Home

When you pick up Yukon from the breeder, bring along a travel crate to carry him to the veterinarian (to check your new acquisition's health) and then home. Even if you have someone else in the car with you, it is a good idea to transport your Northern breed in a crate, rather than have your passenger hold him. A struggling puppy or adult dog can quickly become a dangerous distraction in the car. A travel crate is really the safest means of transporting a dog or puppy.

---

livestock, and kill the neighbors' cats and other small animals. Northern breeds are often not reliable off leash and once set free, are gone for good. Many of these dogs were bred to run for miles. Always keep your Northern breed under control at all times.

Kennels: If you cannot fence in your backyard, consider a prefabricated kennel. Many pet and hardware superstores now carry portable kennel panels that can be installed easily with not much more than a wrench. These come in 6-foot by 6-foot (1.8 m × 1.8 m) panels; you can make Tasha's kennel large or small, depending on the number of panels you purchase. Depending on the size, these kennels will cost from $150 or more.

Many Northern breeds are excellent escape artists, so when you install a kennel or fence, be certain that Yukon can't climb, chew, or dig around it. If your dog is truly an escape artist, you may have to resort to using a kennel with a concrete pad and a sturdy fenced roof. Unless you own a large number of dogs, you should keep your dog inside while you are gone and at night while you sleep.

Tie-outs: What about tie-outs? If you own only one dog and Yukon is strictly a pet, you should not leave him tied out in your backyard. A dog left tied out feels abandoned and can become aggressive. He can become tangled in the chain and become severely injured. Stray dogs can attack him and children can tease him unmercifully.

In Alaska and other northern areas, sled dogs are tied out because deep snow makes kennel runs impractical. These dogs receive attention every day, are frequently exercised, and have each other for company; therefore, tie-outs are not as detrimental to these dogs. If you are a sled dog racer and cannot feasibly kennel all your dogs, then a stakeout system is probably best. However, kennels will protect dogs from predatory wildlife better.

Many Northern breeds tolerate staying outdoors well, if they have adequate shelter and a good water supply. But should you keep your Northern breed outside all the time? Again, if Tasha is strictly a pet, then the answer is an unequivocal "No!" Her place is with you, not alone in a kennel. She will bond more closely to you if she stays inside with you.

Where Your Puppy Should Sleep

Yukon will bond more closely to you if you put his bed in your bedroom. This provides eight hours or more time you are spending with him, even though you are asleep. This will also help reduce his separation anxiety. However, Yukon should have his own bed, preferably in his own crate. The reasons for this are mostly dominance-oriented: Establish now that humans are above dogs. You will help avoid possible dominance problems by enforcing Yukon's sleeping area. Train him that beds are human territory only.

When Yukon cries the first couple of nights, you can rap the crate and tell him to be quiet—all from the comfort of your own bed. If you are a light sleeper, consider you are unlikely to get much sleep the first few nights while both you and Yukon adjust to the new arrangements.

The First Few Hours and Nights

Arrange to have several days at home when you first bring home your Northern breed. If you cannot arrange to take vacation time, try picking Tasha up on a Friday so that you will have the weekend together.

Before you bring her into your house, have her relieve herself outside, then bring her inside to meet family members. Don't let them crowd and overwhelm her; instead, have them individually introduce themselves and give her room to explore. Many new dog and puppy owners often restrict their new pet to a room or two to limit accidents and destructive chewing. You can do this with baby gates or exercise pens. The new surroundings, new people, and new situations will be exhausting and stressful for any puppy or adult dog. Show Tasha her crate, where she will sleep, and perhaps offer her a little food and water. You will want to feed a little less tonight to prevent an upset stomach.

Consider keeping Tasha in a crate at bedtime and while unsupervised, at least until she is housebroken and has proven herself trustworthy alone in the house. With a Northern breed, that may mean never, so it is extremely important that you start crate training early. While humans may look at the crate as a cage, a dog looks upon the crate as a safe haven—a place to hide from the stresses of life. Dogs, especially Northern breeds, have a strong denning instinct. For example, during a thunderstorm, many dog owners find their pet searching for a safe place, usually under a coffee table or bed! A crate, especially an enclosed or covered one makes a dog feel more secure.

Note: Crate training requires a little work on your part. Feed your puppy or dog in her crate. Toss a treat into the crate when you wish her to go in. Use a word such as "*Bed*," "*Crate*," or "*Place*," and give her plenty of praise when she enters the crate. Give her an indestructible chew item or perhaps a small rawhide chew while in the crate to keep her occupied.

TRAINING

If you recall the heritage of the Northern breed dog, the indigenous peoples bred them to pull sleds across frozen tundra. Even the tiny Pomeranian and Alaskan Klee Kai have this instinct, however diluted. Consequently, these dogs were bred to be independent thinkers, capable of spotting bad ice or searching for a blown-in trail. The Inuits often cut these dogs loose to forage for food during the summer months and lean times. These dogs became successful hunters or they starved. They were also required to pull sleds—some were required to haul heavy loads—for long distances, for days on end. Others were used to herd caribou.

Are Northern Breeds Difficult to Train?

The Northern breeds' natural traits—the independent thinking, the tireless pulling, the constant running, and the natural foraging and hunting—made these dogs successful in their harsh environment, but these same traits are often undesirable. Yukon, as an independent thinker, quickly decides that he doesn't want to listen to your commands. Tasha may not understand that you don't want to be dragged down the street like the start of the Iditarod. Yukon may decide that things are far

The indigenous peoples bred Northern breeds to pull sleds across frozen tundra. Even these American Eskimo Dogs have this instinct and consequently are independent thinkers.

more interesting outside your yard and once set free—accidentally or otherwise—may make a mad dash to the next county. Tasha may not differentiate the Thanksgiving turkey on the counter from the kibble in her bowl.

Some traits can be lessened with consistent training; others are too well ingrained for even the best trainer to remedy. It depends largely on the individual dog. Northern breed owners must constantly stay one step ahead of their dog; otherwise, it may lead to serious problems.

Earning Your Northern Breed's Respect

How does one earn a Northern breed's respect?

1. By becoming Alpha—assuming the "boss dog" role. Northern breeds are very pack-oriented, similar to their ancestors, the wolves. In a wolf pack, there is an Alpha male and an

Alpha female—the leaders of the particular wolf pack. These wolves are the ones that often lead the hunt, administer discipline, and breed. By acting as Alpha, Yukon is assured that you are someone to listen to.

2. You must be consistent. Northern breeds require consistent rules. Forbidding Tasha from lying on the couch and then letting her sneak up on it "just this once" will not only confuse her but sends the message that you do not enforce your commands. She will then try breaking other rules to see how far she can go with them.

3. You must not use harsh punishment, nor should you lose your temper. The quickest way to lose Tasha's respect is to yell, hit, kick, or punch her. Beating her will cause her to be fearful and she will never trust you again. Also, the correction must be meaningful for her to understand it. For example, punishing her by withholding her meal for raiding the kitchen counters will *not* work. She will not associate the missed meal with the kitchen counter raid and will actually be more apt to raid the counter because you did not feed her!

4. You should never correct a dog for something she does not understand. Sometimes she will not understand what you are trying to teach her. It is wrong to punish her for not understanding *your* commands. The punishment will confuse her and teach her to be afraid of you, she will not learn what you are trying to teach her.

Routine—a Fundamental Tool

Dogs love routine. It gives them great satisfaction in knowing that dinner will be served promptly at 6:00 P.M. and that walks take place every day at 4:00 P.M.. Schedules and routines are comforting to your pet. They give him some-thing to look forward to. Even if you do not consciously establish a routine, Yukon will notice when you get up and go to sleep and when you feed. Quite often, he may remind you that dinnertime is around the corner as the clock ticks toward the appointed hour.

You can use the schedule to your advantage to train him. For example, if you let him outside to relieve himself first thing in the morning, after breakfast, before you leave for school or work, at noon, when you get home, after dinner, and before bedtime, he will quickly learn to urinate and defecate at these times and that should make housebreaking that much easier. If you crate train, you may find Yukon in his crate right before it is time for him to go to bed!

Rewards and Praise Versus Correction

Positive reinforcement is a popular training technique. Quite simply, it is rewarding behavior that you want to encourage. It makes sense that you should always reward good behavior. Everyone likes praise and rewards. It can be verbal—"What a *Good* Dog!" or tactile—a pat, or it can be a treat. Most Northern breeds respond to food or treats well. A few may not be food-motivated, in which case, you will have to find a motivational object such as a toy.

Likewise, you should never reward bad behavior. For example, if you pet Yukon every time he climbs on you, you are encouraging jumping up. You should also not tolerate behavior that will be annoying or dangerous when your Northern breed is full grown. Mouthing, for example, should not be tolerated in puppies as it can lead to biting when the dog becomes an adult. *Always correct bad behavior.*

What exactly is correction? Correction is not beating a dog or yelling at him. Correction is causing an undesirable behavior to cease. Sometimes it is substituting a correct behavior for the negative one. For example, let's say Yukon has found one of your shoes and is chewing on it. Telling him, "*No! No chew!*" taking the shoe away, and then substituting an appropriate chew item, such as a rawhide bone, is a correction.

Some of the most effective training techniques consist of substituting one behavior for another. For example, suppose Yukon wants to bolt through the door every time you open it. Substituting a *sit-stay* at the door or a *down-stay* on his bed—followed by an appropriate treat—when the doorbell rings can cure "bolting," especially with a food-oriented dog.

Another useful training technique is preventing your Northern breed from exhibiting bad behavior. Yukon can't be bad if you don't let him. Most issues can be resolved with simple foresight. If Yukon has a penchant for running off, the remedy is simple: Don't let him off leash. If he is a destructive chewer, keep him crated or in a kennel when you cannot watch him.

Housebreaking

Housebreaking is easy if you crate train. Most dogs will not soil their beds, so it is natural that puppies and adult dogs will wait to relieve themselves once they are outside the crate. To housebreak your puppy or adult dog, put Yukon outside
✔ when you get up.
✔ after you feed him breakfast.
✔ before you go to school or work.
✔ when you come home at lunchtime.
✔ after the noonday feeding, if applicable.
✔ when you get home from work or school.

TIP

How to Put a Slip or Snap Collar on Your Dog

The slip or snap-type collar should fit without any excess hanging down; if it does, the collar is too big. The collar must be put on properly or when you tighten it, it will not release and can choke your dog. The best way to remember how a slip collar should fit is that it should make a "P" when you hold it over the dog's head. If the "P" is backwards, it will not release.

The correct way to put on a training collar.

✔ after dinner.
✔ after playtime.
✔ before going to bed.

Watch Yukon whenever he is out of his crate. If he starts to sniff around or begins to squat, tell him "*No!*" and rush him outside. He may be so surprised that he may forget he had to go. Give him a few minutes. When he urinates or defecates outside, praise him.

Teaching Your Northern Breed to Not Pull on the Leash

Most Northern breeds pull on the leash; however, you may not want to be dragged around as though you're starting the Iditarod. Introduce Tasha to the training collar first. Put it on her and attach the leash. She may be apprehensive with the new tugging sensation so try luring her with a treat so the collar no longer tightens on her neck. Reward and praise her for calm behavior. If she struggles against the collar, try attaching the leash to her flat collar. Just be sure the flat collar is tight enough and cannot slide over her head if she tries to back out.

The Northern breeds' natural traits—the independent thinking, the tireless pulling, the constant running, and the natural foraging and hunting—made these dogs successful in their harsh environment. A Siberian Husky sled team leaves the starting chute.

After she is confident with the leash and collar, you can start taking her for short walks; she will require some guidance in the direction you are going. Most puppies will tangle around you, trying to find interesting smells, or they will pull wildly. Either way, lure your puppy back with a treat, or you may give her a quick leash correction and continue. Eventually, she will get used to walking on leash.

Once she has accepted the leash, her normal inclination is to pull. When she pulls, try stopping and luring her with a biscuit into a sitting position. Take a few steps with her and if she pulls, lure her back either into a sitting position or backwards a bit so that she is not pulling. Give her a treat when she obeys.

Sometimes your Northern breed pulls so hard that she chokes and gags. Snapping a regular training collar repeatedly can damage the neck and throat. In these extreme circumstances, you may have to use a prong or pinch collar. Unlike regular choke collars, these collars are limited slip and will not choke a dog. They work by pulling the prongs inward and causing pressure on the skin. Most Northern breeds that pull with a regular training collar will not pull with a prong collar. Consult an experienced training professional for the proper fitting and use of a prong collar—incorrect use can result in injury.

The Five Basic Commands

There are five basic commands every Northern breed should know: *heel, sit, down, come,* and *stay.* There are many methods for teaching Tasha these commands; the following use much positive reinforcement. Always have treats in your pocket ready to hand out when she performs correctly.

Sit

Teaching Tasha to *sit* is relatively easy. Have her stand beside your left side with training collar and leash on. With one hand, hold a treat over her nose, just out of reach, and move it backward. With the other hand, lightly push down on her rump and say, "*Tasha, sit!*" Give her the treat when her rump touches the floor. Practice the *sit* often and always reward her when she performs correctly.

Down

Down may be a little more difficult to learn than *sit*. With Yukon standing at your left side with training collar and leash, and have him sit. Hold a treat level with his nose. With a swift movement, bring the treat to the ground closer to Yukon's chest and say, "*Yukon, down!*" He will try to follow the treat and drop to the ground. If he needs help to complete the *down*, you may lightly push on his shoulders. Give him the treat only when he is in the proper *down* position.

Never use the word "down" when you mean "off;" otherwise, Yukon may get confused

Teaching your Northern breed how to sit.

when you put him on a law table and tell him "*Down*." He may jump off because you've been telling him "*Down*" when you meant "*Get off the couch!*"

Heel

Have Tasha sitting beside you on the left side with training collar and leash on. Have a

A Norwegian Buhund doing the work he was bred to do—herding livestock.

The correct method of heeling.

treat in your left hand. Say, "*Tasha, heel!*" and start walking, left foot forward. If Tasha forges ahead or lags behind, get her attention by showing her the treat, and lure her into the correct position. Once in the correct position praise her and give her a treat. If she lags because she is unsure, pat your leg and encourage her to come beside you. Likewise, if she forges ahead, pull her back using the leash or have her focus on the treat and lure her back. Give her the treat when she is in the proper position.

When you stop, have Tasha sit on your left side and give her a treat. When you start again, always start with the left foot forward. Dogs see the left leg movement before the right leg moves. Also, it becomes another signal to your Northern breed that she is to move with you.

Stay

Put Yukon on a leash on your left side and put him in *sit* or *down*. Tell him, "*Yukon, stay!*" and move your outstretched palm in a sweeping motion toward his face. Take one or two steps, *right* foot first, and turn around. If Yukon tries to follow you, say "*No, Yukon, stay!*" and move him back into his original position.

Yukon will eventually stay for a second or two. Before he stands up, give him a treat and quietly praise him, "*Yukon, good stay!*" If he stands, put him back in place. Wait a few seconds and if he stays, give him a treat again. Give him another treat before releasing him. Release him after he stays for 10 seconds. Continue working with him staying for only 10 seconds a few feet away until he has mastered it. Eventually, increase the time to 20 seconds. Give him treats while he is maintaining his *stay*. You will eventually increase distance and time, but do not increase both simultaneously.

You may guess when Yukon will break the *stay* and be able to give him a treat before he does. Anytime Yukon shows nervousness or frequently breaks his *stays*, drop down to a shorter distance and a shorter time so he can have a successful *stay*. Remember: Set up your Northern breed to succeed.

Release Yukon from his *stay* with the word "*Ok.*" Walk over and hug him for doing so well.

Come

Start training *come* by hooking the 6-foot (1.8-m) leather leash to Tasha's collar. Sit Tasha in *heel* position, give her the *stay* command, and go out to the end of the leash. Remember to leave with the right foot! This is an added signal that lets Tasha know she is to stay. Say, "*Tasha, come,*" and give a little tug on the leash. Keep your voice upbeat and happy, not authoritative or angry. If Tasha does not come, reel her in with gentle encouragement. Clap your hands and repeat the command if you have to make Tasha come more willingly. Give her a treat the moment she arrives and make a fuss over her. You may want to teach her to sit in front of you before you reward her.

Once Tasha recalls reliably on a 6-foot leash, start lengthening the distance. You can accomplish this by using a long line, a tracking lead, or a long retractable leash. Practice your recalls around distractions. If Tasha can reliably come when called, you're both ready for the next step.

The next step involves letting your Northern breed think she is off leash. Put a light, long line on her with her leash so that when you take off the regular leash, you still have control, but she is convinced she is off leash. When you do so, practice in a secure area, such as an indoor training facility or a fenced backyard. Start from only 10 feet (3 m) away; gradually lengthening the distance. Once Tasha is reliable in a secure area, move to an unsecured area with many distractions. If you ever have to use the long line, go back to the leash and work on her on-leash recalls.

Problem Behavior

Most problem Nordics become problems because their owners let the situation get out of hand. By their very nature they are inclined to dig, raid garbage cans and countertops, bolt when off leash, and chew on all sorts of inappropriate items. As a Northern breed owner, you should expect this behavior and work toward minimizing it. Don't let Yukon excavate your backyard; don't leave Tasha alone in the kitchen with the roast on the counter.

Digging

Digging is very natural to the Northern breeds. They enjoy digging dens and cooling holes to lie in or to search for small prey. In the winter, digging a hole in snow protects the dog from the elements. This knowledge, however, is little consolation when Tasha has devastated your garden.

Keep Tasha out of areas you do not want her to dig in. That means fencing an area or providing a kennel where you don't care if she digs a hole or two. Filling the holes with her feces and then putting dirt over it sometimes stops her from digging in that spot, but does little to prevent her from digging new holes.

If you can watch Tasha while she is outside, you may want to try the pennies in a pop can method. Take several empty soda cans and put about 5 or 10 pennies in each one and tape the tops. When you see Tasha starting a hole, toss a can so that it hits *near* her. (Do not hit her!) The sound should startle and scare her away from the hole. Wait for a while and continue watching her. If she starts digging a hole again, repeat the procedure. If she doesn't see you hurl the cans, she'll associate the cans being thrown with digging and may decide it is better not to dig. You'll want to pick up the cans when you bring her inside.

If your concern is that she may dig out of your backyard, consider digging a trench at least 6 to 12 inches (15–30 cm) deep under the fence and putting something in to prevent her from getting out. Heavy-gauged mesh fencing, 2-inch (5.1-cm) thick wooden planks,

Most problem Nordics become problems because their owners let the situation get out of hand. A handsome Siberian Husky contemplates his next round of mischief.

or concrete may be enough of a deterrent to stop a dog from digging out. Lining the fence with an electronic wire also works.

Destructive Chewing

Most Northern breeds love to chew. The chew items can be rawhide chews, assorted toys, and "indestructible" nylon bones, or they can be table legs, your IRS return, your new $100 shoes, or a leather sofa. Anything is fair game when you leave a Northern breed alone in your house. Whether or not you've intended it, you've just told Yukon, "Here are your toys—play!"

Keep Yukon crated when you leave the house or when you cannot watch him. If he chooses something inappropriate, offer to "trade" something appropriate and possibly far tastier such as a small rolled rawhide stick or a food treat. Then substitute an appropriate chew item: a marrow bone filled with peanut butter or chew toy, for example.

Sometimes, destructive chewing is associated with separation anxiety.

Countertop and Garbage Raiding

Your Northern breed may force you to become a better housekeeper. Many large Northern breeds have no inhibitions about raiding garbage or countertops. Some develop a fondness for filching anything they can reach. Keeping your countertops clear of enticing items, installing child-proof latches on your cabinets and refrigerator, and hiding the garbage behind a closed door may be the only solution to this problem. The difficulty in training this out lies in the fact that Tasha receives a reward (food or garbage) every time she is successful in her raids. Catching her in the act is difficult and when she learns that she will be corrected, she may become more stealthy. The reward offsets the punishment and she might decide it's worth it.

Trying avoidance techniques like "booby-trapping" the garbage with mousetraps covered with newspaper, or using an electronic static mat are usually ineffective. Most Northern breeds will know the difference between something on a static mat and one not, and many can figure out a dummy mat from a real one!

Running Away

Escape artists are common among the Northern breeds. Most owners of these "Houdini" dogs put up inadequate barriers and their dogs quickly get around them and receive the

Northern breeds are bred to run. Owners must keep these dogs contained or risk losing them. These are Alaskan Huskies.

instant gratification of freedom. Rather than stopping the problem in its tracks, the owners continue to put up poorly thought-out barriers and the dogs continue to escape. The escaping becomes a real problem as the owner puts up increasingly complex barriers, only to have their dog get around them. Houdini dogs have been known to dig through concrete and bend steel-barred wolf cages!

Don't let the problem escalate to this point. Start first by putting up fencing that is dig-proof, climb-proof, and jump-proof. Don't leave your Northern breed outside and unattended for hours with nothing to do. He will use that time to analyze weaknesses in the defense and escape. Instead, keep him busy with a kind of dog playground, such as items that allow him to climb up or go under. Marrow bones or indestructible toys filled with peanut butter or other interesting items will provide hours of enjoyment.

Alleviate the boredom with regular activities. Soon, escaping becomes less of a problem.

This Siberian Husky howls impatiently, waiting to race. Although many do not bark, Northern breeds howl and can disturb nearby neighbors.

Dogs that bolt through doors are similar to Houdini dogs. Stop the behavior by teaching Yukon a new trick. When the doorbell sounds, either put him in his crate with a treat—move the crate closer to the door or purchase a separate one, if necessary—or put him into a *sit-stay* to wait for the treat. Once the door closes again, release Yukon and give him the treat.

Barking and Howling

Don't leave Tasha outside alone during the day or while you sleep. Surprisingly, many owners of nuisance barkers are heavy sleepers and rarely hear their own dogs. If she barks while you are home, try the pennies in a pop can method, as described on page 51. When Tasha starts barking, toss the can so that it hits *near* her. (Do not hit her!) Tell her "*No! Quiet!*" The noise should be enough to startle her.

Anti-bark collars and similar devices are available. Some produce a loud, unpleasant, and distracting noise; these do not always work, especially if your dog enjoys barking. Others work with electric shock, providing a very unpleasant stimulus. There is a new collar on the market that sprays a mist of citronella under the dog's chin. Dogs do not like the spray and cease barking. Of all the antibark collars, this last is probably the most humane and effective.

Shock collar: Use the shock collar only as a last resort. If you choose to use one, use the lowest setting possible. Choose a high-quality collar that reacts to the dog's vocal cords and not just to barking, or your Northern breed may be shocked. Do not leave the collar on her constantly or in wet weather or the prongs may burn the skin. Always use antibarking devices in accordance with the manufacturer's directions.

Nipping

Northern breeds that nip or mouth are not cute. *Never tolerate teeth on your skin for any reason.* It is natural for any puppy to explore its new surroundings; like babies, puppies are eager to inspect things and use their mouths to explore. While this may seem cute and harmless in a puppy, an adult Nordic who mouths is dangerous. Even a nip can break the skin. This is a serious problem that can turn into biting when Yukon is an adult.

If Yukon is a puppy, you can correct mouthing easily. When he begins to mouth you, rap his nose with your index finger and tell him, "*No bite!*" If he insists on chewing on you, hold his lower jaw in your fingers without hurting him and tell him firmly, "*No bite!*" The puppy will usually whine because holding the lower jaw will make him uncomfortable. Release the jaw. If the puppy does not attempt to mouth, give him a treat or toy as a substitution. Tell him, "*Good dog!*" when he accepts the substitute. If he continues to mouth, repeat the above procedures. Usually, a few times is enough for Yukon to get the idea.

If Yukon is an adult and mouths, you can try the same techniques, but remember that an adult may behave very differently from a puppy. An adult that mouths, grabs clothing, or bites at hands and feet is a serious problem. Consult a professional trainer.

Dominance and Aggression

Dominance problems arise when you as the owner are unable to control your Northern breed. Dominance may be displayed through aggression or growling when you try to push Tasha off the couch or touch her while she eats. Other signs of dominance include leg mounting, urinating on your bed or other furniture, and other negative behavior. Should Tasha behave in this fashion, first contact your veterinarian to be certain the problem is not biological. Some dogs with hidden injuries or conditions may snap when you try to pet them because they are in pain. If the problem is not medical, you should then contact a dog behavior specialist, one that has experience with Northern breeds and dominance problems.

Chasing/Killing Small Animals— the Prey Drive

Most Northern breeds love to chase and kill small animals. Many a squirrel, rodent, or cat have strayed into a Northern breed's backyard and become a snack. Unfortunately, there is little you can do to change this prey drive. As a Northern breed owner, you must watch for it and stop the behavior before it starts.

Take Yukon walking on leash. If he sees a small animal and tries to pursue it, stop him with a "No!" and give him a *sit* command. After he sits, give him a treat. Every time you see a small animal you know he would like to chase, put him in a *sit*, let the animal pass, and then give Yukon a treat. He may learn this quickly and you may find him sitting on his own whenever a squirrel goes by! Even so, Yukon is most likely untrustworthy off leash and will revert to hunting.

Socialize Yukon with children and cats while he is still a puppy. He will quickly learn that children are small humans and not animals. Most Northern breeds, once socialized with children, can make the distinction. You should always supervise these visits, as puppies can be rambunctious. Children can also hurt a puppy, causing it to bite or snap.

Dog Aggression

Some Northern breeds are dog-aggressive, but many can and do get along with other dogs. Most dog aggression occurs because of dominance issues and pack hierarchy.

If Tasha gets in a fight, do not let her "fight it out" with the other dog—you may end up with a dead dog! Use whatever means possible to break up the fight. A garden hose or pepper spray may be effective.

Never wade into a dog fight or you are very likely to get bitten. If you decide to take that chance, then be extremely careful, as even a medium-sized dog can crunch bone. If both you and the owner of the other dog can grasp the dogs' collars safely without getting bitten, do so and haul the dogs away. Grabbing a tail or flank may cause the dog to wheel around and bite you.

If Tasha displays signs of dog aggression, such as starting fights, do not try to correct this yourself. Go to a professional dog trainer who has experience in handling such dogs.

Dog food isn't what it used to be. Premium dog food from even 10 years ago can't compare nutritionally with today's products. Many premium dog foods are more digestible, have better protein and fat sources, and even include supplements such as Omega-3 fatty acids, glucosamine, and probiotics. Dog owners largely have the sled dog and Northern breeds to thank for these nutritional advances. Mushers, trying to find the optimal nutrition for their working dogs, allowed research on their canine athletes so veterinarians and canine nutritionists could formulate an ideal nutrition.These studies, plus intensive feeding trials and research, culminated in the development of many premium dog foods. The adult dog or maintenance versions are slightly altered renditions of the performance kibble that the working dogs eat.

The Right Dog Food for Your Northern Breed

When you choose a dog food, always purchase a recognizable premium brand—*recognizable* because it is easily obtained. This is important when it is 9:00 P.M. and you've just run out of dog food. Worse yet, you don't want to search all over town if the pet bou-

Your Northern breed will benefit from a diet of premium dog food. This Keeshond is the picture of optimum health and good nutrition.

tique next door stops carrying your brand! *Premium* because you don't have to feed as much, it is more digestible, and has more nutrition.

Is there a difference between premium dog food and bargain brands? Yes! Premium brands often use higher-quality ingredients that are more digestible than bargain brands. Dogs can often digest and use meat and by-products in premium brands much easier than the cheaper dog foods, although the bargain brands tout the same protein and fat levels. If you compare the ingredients, you'll find bargain brands filled with cheap sources of protein such as soy and bonemeal, as well as fillers, sugar, salt, and

Vegetarian Diets

Vegetarian diets are not suitable for Northern breeds. Most Northern breeds require higher protein from a good meat source and many are allergic to soy, which is the primary protein source, for vegetarian diets. Dogs are carnivores and process meat more efficiently. If you work your Northern breed, be certain to feed her a good meat-based diet. Vegetarian diets cannot meet the protein requirements of a working dog.

artificial colors and flavors. The amount of money you "save" by purchasing bargain brands is often offset by the amount of dog food necessary to feed to obtain the same nutrition as a premium brand. Sometimes you must feed as much as two to three times the amount of bargain brand dog food to obtain the same nutrition as a premium brand dog food. Not much of a bargain, is it?

Choose a good adult or maintenance dog food if Yukon is a pet. Most active Northern breeds need about 26 percent protein and 15 percent fat-by-weight dog food. A percentage or two on either side is all right. If Tasha works in a sled team, consider a 30 percent protein and 20 percent fat-by-weight diet.

Whichever premium brand of food you choose, it should state that it meets the guidelines as set forth by the Association of American Feed Control Officials committee. AAFCO has established guidelines for dogs' and puppies' nutritional needs. Most major dog food companies comply with AAFCO guidelines, but you should check regardless of the brand or manufacturer.

Choose a dog food with a meat source such as chicken or poultry, beef, lamb, or turkey, or by-products. By-products, depending on the ingredients, can actually be a better source of nutrition than meat.

Feeding Your Northern Breed

✔ Puppies under four months—Feed three times a day.
✔ Puppies over four months and adults—Feed twice daily.

Follow the recommendations on the premium puppy or dog food package on amounts and split into portions. Most dog food manufacturers recommend more dog food than a Northern breed needs, so adjust accordingly. Feed Tasha a premium puppy food until she reaches one year of age; after that, you should feed her an adult premium dog food.

If Yukon picks at his food or does not eat within ten minutes, pick up the food and offer it to him at his next mealtime. Do not add table scraps or give him treats to tide him over, or you will make him a picky eater. You are teaching him good eating habits by insisting that he eat when you offer food.

Nutritional Requirements for the Working Dog

Most working dogs benefit from a higher protein and fat diet such as the amounts in a premium performance dog food. If Yukon works hard, such as running in a sled team more than twice a week or twice a week for long distances—over 20 miles (32 km) at a time, you may notice that a premium dog food may not be enough.

Most sled dog racers supplement with meat, fat, vitamins, and minerals to keep their sled dogs at peak performance. Many use premixed frozen meat such as Champaign Race Diet along with the premium dog food to provide a balanced diet. If you are planning on working your dog hard, you may wish to consider using these race formulas.

✔ Working dogs require higher protein and fat levels than pets. The dog's body uses protein for building muscle and repairing injuries. Dogs on a lower protein diet are more apt to become injured than those on a higher protein dog food. Generally, a working dog should have a diet that consists of 25 to 35 percent of its calories from protein.

✔ Working dogs use fat as an energy source more efficiently than carbohydrates. A high-fat/lower-carbohydrate diet helps dogs work at their peak efficiency. The best fats come from animal sources. Generally, a working dog should have a diet that consists of 40 to 60 percent of its calories from fat. A caveat to this is Omega-3 fatty acids, which are relatively new, but have recently received a lot of press. Research suggests that these fats help reduce inflammation, lower blood pressure, and may even shrink certain types of tumors. However, too much is a bad thing. They can inhibit blood clotting, which can lead to hemorrhaging; therefore, you should feed no more than 5 percent of total fat calories in Omega-3s.

✔ Carbohydrates play a role in the working dog's diet, especially during recovery. Within 20 minutes after an anaerobic workout, dogs can benefit from receiving a soupy drink or meat mixed with glucose polymers. These simple carbohydrates will help replete a dog's glycogen stores, the energy store within the cell's mitochondria. This will help in recovery time.

There are several good commercial glycogen replacement supplements on the market. Hydrolyzed cornstarch, available through feed stores, can provide a low-cost glucose polymer. Either DE-12 or DE-15 will work. The rule is 1 gram per pound (.45 kg) of body weight or about 2 ounces (56 g) for a 50-pound (23-kg) dog. Do not use fructose-based sports drinks made for humans as they can send a dog into insulin shock. If you do feed it, give it in water, mixed with a little lean broth. (Do not mix the glycogen replacement with fat; fat tends to hinder absorption.) You must feed the glucose polymer within 20 minutes after the dog has completed exercising.

It takes at least six weeks or longer before you will see any effect due to a diet change. Plan Yukon's diet so that he can benefit from it before you need him to work. Many mushers keep their dogs on the same diet year-round to avoid possibly affecting performance.

Mix Your Own or Purchase?

You've decided that Tasha could benefit from a better diet than the diet that is available commercially. Before you mix up your own version of witch's brew, reconsider your decision. Many working dogs are able to work quite well on a premium high-performance dog food. Many top sled dog teams are able to feed a high-quality premium formula and a frozen or dehydrated complete meat supplement without mixing their own. Consider these options first before trying to concoct your own diet.

If you cannot obtain a balanced meat supplement or it is prohibitively expensive, first

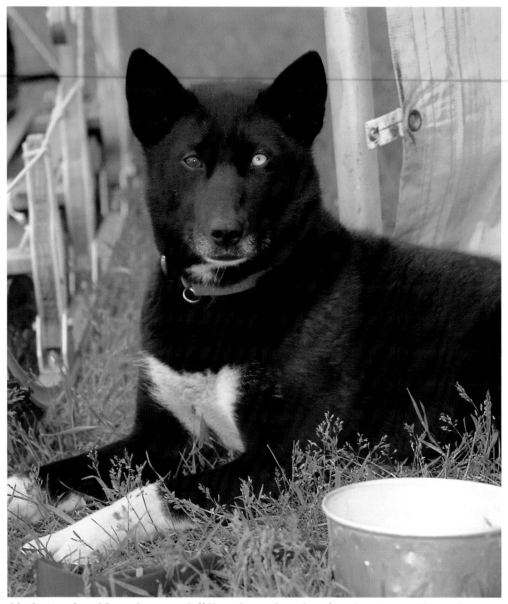

Mushers such as Iditarod winner, Jeff King, know the value of good nutrition. This is Cannon, an Alaskan Husky leader on King's team.

Working dogs benefit from a higher protein and fat diet. These are Alaskan Huskies.

contact a canine nutritionist at a veterinary college to help you formulate your own dog food. This may be an expensive way to go, as you may have to pay for feed analysis and other tests, but it will help ensure that you have no imbalances in your diet. They can greatly affect your dog's performance or can even cause severe health problems. Calcium and phosphorus, for example, can cause severe bone problems if greatly out of balance.

Home Diets

What about home-cooked diets for the pet? Dog food has made significant advances in nutrition within the past 20 years due to intensive research. Unless you are a canine

If you choose to mix your own food, contact a canine nutritionist at a veterinary college to help you formulate your own working dog diet. This Siberian Husky benefits from an optimal diet.

nutritionist or have done extensive research into canine nutrition, it is highly unlikely that anything you could put together would be balanced or provide all the necessary nutrients for your dog. Dog food undergoes extensive testing to be certain of the quality and the nutritional content of the food.

If you do decide to cook your own dog food, consult with a veterinarian who has experience in developing homemade diets.

Water

We don't tend to think of water as a nutrient because it is commonplace, but it is actually the most vital nutrient for life. Dogs can live for days without food, but can die from dehydration in as little as 24 hours. A slightly dehydrated dog will show a marked decrease in performance running on a sled team.

Overweight Northern Breeds

Contrary to popular belief, a chubby puppy is not a healthy one. Neither puppies nor adults should be fat. Obesity can cause problems with joint and bone formation and can stress your puppy. You can determine Yukon's condition by placing your thumbs on his spine and using your fingers to feel his ribs. If you can't feel his ribs or spine, or have a hard time feeling them through the fat, you must cut back his food.

Some people have difficulty limiting their dog's food. If you are one of these tender-hearted souls, feed Yukon the maintenance or "lite" equivalent of his normal food or consult with your veterinarian for a specific diet. Increasing his exercise will also help to shave off unwanted weight.

Dogs can become dehydrated at any time of the year, including winter. Snow has very little moisture and is not a suitable water supply. During the summer months, you should always have a fresh water source available. During the winter months, dogs tend to drink less and water freezes in areas where the temperature dips below 32°F (0°C).

Mushers combat dehydration by "baiting" the dogs' drinking water, adding meat, dog food, or other enticing foods to make a warm soup, and offering it to their sled dogs twice daily. The dogs learn to drink their water in the morning and eat their food soaked with warm water in the evening. If you have multiple dogs, this may be the most economical solution if you live in areas where the temperatures frequently stay below the freezing point.

Check for dehydration to determine if you are giving Tasha enough water. Pull up the skin at the back of her neck and let it snap back. If it snaps back quickly, the dog usually is well hydrated; if it "melts" back or stays where it is, the dog is dehydrated.

If you have one or two dogs, or can afford it, the best way to provide fresh water year-round is with an electric bucket or bowl water heater. These devices keep the water above freezing temperatures, ensuring that your dogs have water always available. A major drawback to these water heaters is that you must always have the heater plugged into an electrical outlet. If Yukon is a destructive chewer, he could bite into an exposed cord section and become electrocuted. Likewise, if you have many dogs or have your dog's kennel far from an electrical outlet, it may be impractical to use a heated water bowl.

Nutrition Chart for Northern Breeds in Cups Per Day

Size of Breed/Age
Regular Activity (Normal activity)
Active (Hiking/Showing)
High Performance/Working (Sledding, skijoring)

Small/Puppy (age 8 weeks to 12 months)
Pomeranian, German Spitz, Shiba Inu, Norwegian Puffin Dog
- .75–1.5 cup puppy food
- 1–2 cups puppy food
- 2–3 cups puppy food

Medium/Puppy (age 8 weeks to 12 months)
Siberian Husky, Alaskan Husky, Samoyed
- 1–2 cups puppy food
- 2–3 cups puppy food
- 3–4 cups puppy food

Large/Puppy (age 8 weeks to 12 months)
Alaskan Malamute, Akita Inu, Canadian Inuit Dog
- 2–3 cups puppy food
- 3–4 cups puppy food
- 4–5 cups puppy food

Small/Adult (age 12 months to 6 years)
Pomeranian, German Spitz, Shiba Inu, Norwegian Puffin Dog
- .75–1.5 cup adult or maintenance food
- 1–2 cups adult food
- 2–3 cups performance food
*May need to supplement with a balanced meat mixture

Medium/Adult (age 12 months to 6 years)
Siberian Husky, Alaskan Husky, Samoyed
- 1–2 cups adult or maintenance food
- 2–3 cups adult food
- 3–4 cups performance food
*May need to supplement with a balanced meat mixture

Large/Adult (age 12 months to 6 years)
Alaskan Malamute, Akita Inu, Canadian Inuit Dog
- 2–3 cups adult or maintenance food
- 3–4 cups adult food
- 4–5 cups performance food
*May need to supplement with a balanced meat mixture

Small/Adult (age 7 years +) Pomeranian, German Spitz, Shiba Inu, Norwegian Puffin Dog
- .75–1.5 cup adult, maintenance, or senior food
- 1–2 cups adult or senior food
- 2–3 cups adult or performance food
*May need to supplement with a balanced meat mixture

Medium/Adult (age 7 years +) Siberian Husky, Alaskan Husky, Samoyed
- 1–2 cups adult, maintenance, or senior food
- 2–3 cups adult or senior food
- 3–4 cups adult or performance food
*May need to supplement with a balanced meat mixture

Large/Adult (age 12 months to 6 years)
Alaskan Malamute, Akita Inu, Canadian Inuit Dog
- 2–3 cups adult or maintenance food
- 3–4 cups adult or senior food
- 4–5 cups adult or performance food
*May need to supplement with a balanced meat mixture

*NOTE: These are only guidelines for feeding. Your dog may benefit from more or less food depending on his actual condition, metabolism, and activity level.

Depending on the breed, most Nordic dogs need a moderate to intensive amount of grooming. They do not need clipping and intensive bathing like as single-coated breeds do, but their double coats require frequent brushing and combing. A double-coated breed is a dog with longer, harsh guard hairs and a downy undercoat. This specialized coat differentiates the Nordic dogs from single-coat breeds such as Poodles and Cocker Spaniels. Long-haired breeds, such as Keeshonden and dogs with woolly coats, require intensive brushing and combing to prevent mats, whereas shorter-coated dogs may get by with less frequent groomings.

Grooming the Northern Breed

All Northern breeds shed or "blow coat" twice yearly. During this time, a Northern breed's coat literally comes out in handfuls; you may find yourself overwhelmed by the sheer amount of hair during this shedding period.

As a rule, never bathe Yukon before brushing and combing him out. If he has mats, they will become more difficult to get out. Instead, comb out your Northern breed and then bathe him. The only exception to this rule is when your Northern breed is blowing coat, when bathing

Depending on the breed, most Nordic dogs require a moderate to intensive amount of grooming. A Shiba Inu with a beautiful coat.

him in lukewarm water will help loosen the dead hair and will facilitate shedding.

There are varieties of different grooming implements available. Unless you plan to show Tasha in conformation, you need only a minimal amount of equipment to groom her. One useful piece of equipment is the grooming table. It enables you to work on Tasha at a comfortable height and allows you access to her at any angle.

Brushing and Combing

Most Northern breed owners can get by with brushing and combing their dog twice weekly, but daily is preferable—more often during the twice-a-year shedding. If your Northern breed is a woolly or has an exceptionally long coat that is prone to tangles, you may have to brush and comb more frequently.

When you begin brushing and combing Tasha, start by using the slicker brush to remove all loose and dead hair. Brush her along the normal lay of her hair and then brush against the grain. After brushing her hair backwards, brush it back to its normal lay. You can then comb out the hair at this time.

If Tasha has mats or is shedding, use a mat rake to remove the undercoat, then brush and comb as normal.

Bathing

Brush and comb your Northern breed to remove excess hair and prevent matting. Run a lukewarm or tepid bath—hot water can burn your dog. You may put some cotton balls in her ears to prevent water getting inside them before you place her in the tub. Do not stuff the cotton deep into the ear canal, however; this can damage the eardrum or be difficult to remove.

Always use a shampoo and creme rinse specifically made for dogs. Do not use human shampoo as it has the wrong pH and may be too harsh on the fur and skin. Soak Tasha thoroughly, lather her up, and then rinse well. Repeat if she is very dirty. Use a conditioner or creme rinse made for dogs to prevent tangles and rinse well; any leftover soap or conditioner will attract dirt. In extreme cases, the dried residue will irritate the skin.

Use thick terry cloth towels to dry Tasha and then use a blow dryer made for dogs. *Do not use human hair dryers!* They are too hot and can burn your Northern breed or damage her coat. Also, be very careful with cage dryers; some dogs have overheated and died because of their improper use.

Trimming Nails

Trim Tasha's nails weekly to keep them short. You can use either an electric nail grinder or a dog nail clippers. Northern breeds may have either black or light-colored nails. If any of Tasha's nails are light-colored, look at them closely. You will see a pink fleshy part where the blood supply and nerves are. This is called the *quick* and if you cut into it, it will cause the dog a great deal of pain and will bleed profusely.

To trim Tasha's nails, hold a paw firmly and carefully snip off a sliver of nail. (You may also use a nail grinder to grind the toenail down). Remove a little at a time, especially if you cannot determine where the quick is. If the nail feels spongy or soft, stop cutting immediately. If you cut the quick, pack the nail with styptic powder immediately.

If you have let Tasha's nails overgrow, you can cause the quick to shrink by trimming the nail up to the quick every two to three days. The quick will naturally recede, allowing you to remove more of the nail the next time.

Grooming Equipment

✔ Slicker brush
✔ Long-toothed comb
✔ Mat rake
✔ Undercoat rake
✔ Mat splitter
✔ Grooming table
✔ Nail clippers or nail grinder and styptic powder
✔ Dog hair dryer
✔ Shampoo and creme rinse made especially for dogs

Spaying and Neutering

Should you spay or neuter your pet? The answer in most cases is yes, unless your Northern breed is purebred and show quality or proven as a superior performance dog. Every year, about five million pets are euthanized at shelters. Many are purebred dogs, including Northern breeds.

Besides not contributing to the burgeoning pet overpopulation, spaying or neutering your pet has many health benefits, including preventing or reducing the risk to many types of cancers and tumors. In many cases, behavior problems disappear when you spay or neuter your pet. Overall, you will have happier, healthier pet.

Vaccinations

Vaccinations protect your dog from deadly diseases such as rabies, parvovirus, and distemper. Young puppies and elderly dogs are more susceptible to diseases than adult dogs, but any dog may contract and die from these diseases. If you purchased your Northern breed puppy from a reputable breeder, she should have her first series of vaccinations. If Tasha is an adult, the breeder should have had her vaccinated against all diseases. The breeder should provide you with a vaccination record indicating the date of the vaccinations and the type of vaccination given.

Follow your veterinarian's advice concerning vaccinations. If Yukon is at high risk for a contagious disease due to frequent contact with strange dogs, such as at a dog show or sled dog race, consider an aggressive vaccination schedule.

Internal Parasites

Internal parasites include worms such as roundworms and hookworms, but can also

▬ CHECKLIST ▬

Benefits to Spaying and Neutering Your Northern Breed

1 Reduces or eliminates the risk of certain types of cancers and tumors including (for males) prostate and testicular; (for females) mammary, uterine, and ovarian.

2 Eliminates the urge to roam to look for mates.

3 Prevents unwanted litters; makes you a responsible owner.

4 Can reduce aggression in both sexes.

5 Eliminates the risk of the female contracting pyometra, a potentially fatal condition where the uterus becomes infected.

6 In females, eliminates the heat cycle, which can occur as frequently as once every three months.

7 Can make your Northern breed more attentive and responsive to you; can help eliminate behavioral problems.

include parasites such as Giardia and Coccidia. Some worms feed off intestinal contents, depriving the dog of vital nutrition. Worms such as hookworms can cause severe anemia by feeding off your dog's blood. Heartworms live in the dog's heart and blood and can kill a dog. Giardia

All Northern breeds shed or "blow coat" twice yearly. These are Chinooks.

and other single-cell parasites will cause severe diarrhea and weight loss.

Worms

The most common worms are roundworms, hookworms, and tapeworms. Roundworms or ascarids and tapeworms, to a lesser extent, feed on food as it passes through the intestines, robbing your dog of the nutrition he needs. Hookworms attach themselves to the lower intestines and feed on your dog's blood. In severe infestations, hookworms can actually kill a dog.

Most breeders will worm their puppies before sending them home, but you should have your puppy rechecked for further infestations. If you suspect that Yukon has worms, take a fecal sample to your veterinarian for analysis. Do not use over-the-counter dewormers as many are ineffective against certain types of worms.

Heartworms: The heartworm is an internal parasite that can kill your dog. Mosquitoes transmit heartworms by feeding on an infected dog. The microfilariae or heartworm larvae from the infected dog incubate within the mosquito for several days. When the infected mosquito feeds off another dog, it injects the infectious microfilariae into the dog and he becomes infected with heartworm.

You should put Yukon on a heartworm preventative, if you live in a heartworm area. Most states within the continental United States have heartworms, although it is less prevalent in the western states.

Fleas and Ticks

Fleas are more than just annoying hard-shelled insects that feed on blood and make your dog miserable. Fleas are carriers of bubonic plague, which can severely affect your dog's health. Fleas thrive in all climates except the very cold, the very dry, and high altitudes. You can search for fleas on Tasha around her belly and groin area, at the base of her tail, and around her ears. A common sign of fleas are deposits of black flea feces that turn red when wet.

If you find fleas on Tasha, you can guarantee that you have a flea infestation in your home. Talk to your veterinarian about ways to combat the problem. Often, your veterinarian can recommend a system that will combat fleas in the yard, in your house, and on your dog.

Ticks are insects that carry dangerous diseases such as Rocky Mountain spotted fever, Lyme disease, and ehrlichiosis. If you find a tick on Yukon, avoid handling it or you may risk exposing yourself to these diseases. Instead, treat the area with a good tick insecticide approved for use on dogs, wait a few minutes, and then try to remove it. Wear latex gloves and use tweezers. Firmly grasp the tick with the tweezers and gently pull. Don't try to pull the tick out if it resists. You may leave portions of the tick embedded in your dog, which may become infected. Wait for the tick to drop off and dispose of it.

Hereditary and Congenital Problems in the Northern Breeds

Bloat

Bloat is the common name for a life-threatening condition called gastric dilatation, gastric torsion, or canine gastric dilatation-volvulus (CGDV). Bloat commonly affects deep-chested breeds such as Siberian Huskies and Alaskan Malamutes. Larger breeds are more prone to bloat than smaller ones.

In bloat, the stomach rapidly fills with gas, putting pressure on internal organs. If the bloat is severe, the stomach turns on its axis

If your Northern breed has an exceptionally long coat, such as this Finnish Lapphund, you may have to brush and comb daily.

and becomes gastric torsion or volvulus. Shock and death follow. Dogs that bloat suddenly look pregnant or fat. The dog may pace back and forth and appear to be in pain. He may drool excessively and seem uncomfortable when he sits or lies down. He may retch in an attempt to vomit. *Bloat is a serious life-threatening condition*—obtain emergency veterinary care immediately. Do not attempt to treat this yourself.

To help prevent bloat, try feeding several smaller meals instead of one large one. Don't suddenly change foods or add extra tidbits that might cause stomach upsets. Adding water to dry food aids in its evacuation from the stomach. Bloat occurs within three hours after feeding, so don't feed and leave. Watch your Northern breed closely for any sign of distress after eating.

Elbow Dysplasia

Elbow dysplasia is a hereditary disease in which the dog's elbow joints are malformed. As with hip dysplasia, no amount of nutrition or supplements will prevent it. If your particular Northern breed is susceptible to elbow dysplasia, is very important to have his parents certified with the OFA (Orthopedic Foundation for Animals) as free of elbow dysplasia. The elbow dysplasia certification is not as common as the hip dysplasia, possibly because breeders may be unaware of the need to certify their dogs. Certification requires an X ray and certification through OFA.

Entropion and Ectropion

Entropion is a hereditary condition in which the eyelid turns inward into the eye, causing the eyelashes and fur to rub against the eye-ball. It is obviously irritating to the dog and usually requires surgery to correct. Ectropion is where the lower eyelid droops, exposing its interior. In mild cases, your veterinarian may prescribe eyedrops and antibiotic and corticosteroid ophthalmic ointment. In severe cases, surgery may be required.

Hip Dysplasia

Hip dysplasia is a hereditary canine disease that affects the formation of the hips. Hip dysplasia affects all breeds and no amount of nutrition will affect it. In mildly dysplastic cases, your veterinarian may be able to mitigate it with antiinflammatories such as Rimadyl or aspirin, or nutritional aids such as glucosamine, chondroitin, and creatine. Serious cases may require expensive surgery. Some extreme cases of hip dysplasia may be so painful that the humane thing to do is to euthanize the dog.

Dogs are certified clear of hip dysplasia through OFA. The dog must be two years old or older to have OFA certify his hips. A veterinarian X-rays the dog's hips and sends the X rays to OFA. An approved veterinarian then determines whether the dog's hips are Excellent, Good, Fair, or Poor. The dog is considered free from hip dysplasia if he has an Excellent, Good, or Fair rating. Many breeders will not breed a dog with hips less than a Good rating.

Hypothyroidism

Hypothyroidism is a condition in which the dog's thyroid produces insufficient levels of thyroid hormone. Dogs with hypothyroidism tend to be overweight, have a dull and dry coat, and may have a lower tolerance to cold. Some dogs' coats thin and look "burned out."

Hypothyroidism can cause infertility in intact males and females.

A simple blood test will diagnose whether a dog is hypothyroid or not. Some forms of hypothyroidism may be hereditary, so it is important to have your dog's breeder screen for hypothyroidism. OFA has a thyroid registry but it is relatively new, so some breeders may not be aware of it. If your Northern breed is hypothyroid, your veterinarian may prescribe a form of thyroid hormone.

Progressive Retinal Atrophy (PRA), Central Progressive Retinal Atrophy (CPRA), and Cataracts

PRA and CPRA are two degenerative eye disorders that lead to blindness. Cataracts or cloudiness of the eye's lens can be due to either hereditary or environmental reasons. Juvenile cataracts are usually hereditary.

A veterinary opthamologist can determine whether your Northern breed has these or other eye diseases. The Canine Eye Registry Foundation (CERF) provides a registry for dogs intended for breeding. The CERF evaluation lasts for one year. Any Northern breed that you buy should have both its parents registered with CERF.

Chondrodysplasia (CHD)

Chondrodysplasia or "dwarfism" affects breeds such as the Alaskan Malamute and Canadian Inuit Dog. It is a genetic disease that causes the malformation of the carpal and radius bones, which makes the dog's forelimbs appear stunted. Puppies born with this disease do not display outward signs of CHD until much later, although X rays up until the age of three months can confirm chondrodysplasia.

There is no cure for CHD, nor is there any surgery available to correct this condition. If severe and painful, the only humane choice you may have is to euthanize the dog.

There is no definitive test for carriers of CHD, although the Alaskan Malamute Club of America (AMCA) is currently working on a genetic test for it. AMCA has a CHD certification that is not 100 percent, but it is better than no certification. If you purchase an Alaskan Malamute puppy, have the puppy's forelimbs X-rayed or make certain that the parents have a CHD rating lower than 6.25 percent from AMCA.

Zinc Dermatitis

Zinc dermatitis is a relatively newly discovered condition that tends to affect many Northern breeds. It usually appears similar to a scaly "sunburned" nose, although the ears, eyelids, muzzle, genitals, and paw pads may be scaly as well. A veterinarian can easily misdiagnose zinc dermatitis as pemphigus, "collie nose," or another type of autoimmune problem. This condition occurs when the dog's body does not absorb enough zinc in his diet. Changing to a different food does not affect the condition; supplementing with zinc does. You veterinarian can diagnose zinc dermatitis through a biopsy. Dogs with zinc dermatitis should not be bred, as it may be genetic in origin.

Anesthesia Sensitivity

Most Northern breeds may exhibit sensitivity to anesthesia similar to sighthounds. These dogs may have difficulty coming out of the anesthesia or may have other detrimental effects, due to the low body fat that many

Northern breeds exhibit. Because of this sensitivity, your veterinarian must take appropriate precautions.

Common Illnesses

Diarrhea

Diarrhea has many causes including viruses, bacteria, strange food, stress, and others. If your Northern breed has severe diarrhea, that is, diarrhea that is accompanied by fever—over 102°F (38.9°C)—vomiting, or dehydration, or has diarrhea that contains blood or mucus, seek veterinary attention. Serious medical conditions such as parvovirus, distemper, food poisoning, or Giardia can also cause diarrhea.

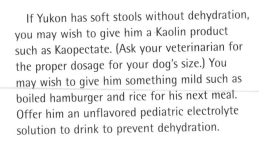

If Yukon has soft stools without dehydration, you may wish to give him a Kaolin product such as Kaopectate. (Ask your veterinarian for the proper dosage for your dog's size.) You may wish to give him something mild such as boiled hamburger and rice for his next meal. Offer him an unflavored pediatric electrolyte solution to drink to prevent dehydration.

Vomiting

Dogs vomit for a variety of reasons. If Tasha vomits more than twice in 12 hours, projectile vomits, starts becoming dehydrated, has a fever with the vomiting, retches without vomiting, or has diarrhea with her vomiting, bring her to the veterinarian immediately. She may have a more serious condition such as parvovirus, enlarged esophagus, an obstruction, or Giardia.

If Tasha has vomited but does not show any other signs of illness, consider withholding her food for a few hours. Sometimes an over-the-counter antacid such as Pepto Bismol helps coat the stomach. (Consult your veterinarian for the proper usage of medications.) Offer her unflavored pediatric electrolyte solution to drink to prevent dehydration. Then feed her boiled rice and hamburger. If she does not vomit it up, you can feed her normally at her next mealtime.

Dogs such as the Shar-pei and the Chow Chow may develop eyelid problems such as entropion. This is a smooth coat Chow Chow.

Lumps and Bumps on the Skin

Most lumps and bumps are usually benign sebaceous cysts, but you should show any lump or bump to your veterinarian, especially if it is red, oozing, dark colored, irregular in size and shape, or fast growing. If your female Northern breed has lumps on her mammary glands, have a veterinarian examine her immediately. A large doughy lump on the stomach might be a hernia that your veterinarian may have to fix.

Broken Toenails

Most broken toenails occur when you allow your dog's nails to grow too long. If Yukon has a broken or cracked toenail below the quick,

Left: Hip dysplasia affects all purebreds and mixed breeds. Your dog's parent should be certified free from hip dysplasia through OFA. Shown is a Chinese Shar-pei.

Above: This Finnish Lapphund is the picture of perfect health.

file or grind it down. If the toenail is bleeding, pack it with styptic powder to stop the bleeding, then coat it with a surgical bond agent, available through most veterinary supply houses. Occasionally, a dog may actually rip off a nail. In this case, staunch the bleeding and seek veterinary attention.

Ear Problems

Yukon's ears should be clean smelling and free of debris and waxy buildup. There should be no sign of redness. Clean your dog's ears once weekly with an over-the-counter, mild otic solution. If he paws at his ears or shakes his head, he may have an ear infection or a mite infestation. In this case, do not use an over-the-counter mite solution as this may irritate the ear more. Your veterinarian can prescribe a medication for Yukon's ears.

Skin Problems

Hot spots and "collar rot": "Hot spots" are areas of moist dermatitis. They usually occur due to some type of irritation and can erupt in just a few hours. They are red, often feel hot to the touch, and can quickly become infected. "Collar rot" is the term for hot spots that appear under collars. This sometimes occurs with sled dogs that are staked out or are in a kennel. The hair beneath the collar becomes matted and irritates the skin.

Clip all hair around the hot spot and gently clean it with a 10 percent betadine/90 percent water solution. Dry the area thoroughly. If it becomes infected or if the hot spots are extensive, you may have to bring your dog to the veterinarian to have them cleaned. Your veterinarian may prescribe antibiotics.

You can prevent collar rot by either washing or replacing your dogs' collars once a year. Don't keep the collar too tight, and be certain to brush or massage the hair under the collar at least weekly to prevent matting.

Mange: Mange mites can cause itching and hair loss. The two common types of mange are sarcoptic and demodectic. Sarcoptic mange causes intense itching. Demodectic causes severe hair loss. Both must be diagnosed through skin scrapings and treated through a veterinarian. Over-the-counter remedies seldom work well.

Ringworm: Ringworm, a fungus, usually affects puppies. Most adult dogs are fairly resistant to it, but a virulent ringworm infection can affect adults. It is contagious to both humans and cats, so wear latex gloves when treating it.

Ringworm often appears as a bald patch of skin. If you do not treat it, it will grow and spread. You can treat most localized ringworm infections with a solution of 10 percent betadine and 90 percent water. Antibacterial and antifungal shampoos with povidone-iodine, made for dogs, work reasonably well. Bathe Yukon in the antifungal shampoo and then treat the localized ringworm with the betadine-water solution. Continue treating the ringworm patch with the betadine-water solution until it clears up. If the ringworm continues to spread, even with treatment, your veterinarian may have to prescribe Fulvin (Griseofulvin). This treatment is moderately expensive, somewhat toxic, and may take up to one to three months to cure.

Fly bites: Flies will torment your Northern breed mercilessly. Fly strikes usually occur on ears and face where the skin is most vulnerable. If allowed to continue, flies can actually damage skin and in extreme cases, Yukon could lose part of his ears. Use a mild, roll-on fly ear ointment that can be used in conjunction with any flea and tick pesticides you normally use. Some systemic insecticides do a good job at repelling flies, although the product may not list it as a fly repellent.

CHECKLIST

Assembling a First Aid Kit

Every household with a dog should have a first aid kit. You can assemble one from easily purchasable items:

✔ Large and small nonstick bandage pads

✔ Sterile gauze wrappings

✔ Sterile sponges

✔ Pressure bandages

✔ Self-adhesive wrap (VetWrap)

✔ Disposable latex gloves

✔ Triple antibiotic ointment or nitrofurizone—Nitrofurizone is available through veterinary supply catalogs—for cuts and wounds

✔ Bandage tape

✔ Surgical glue or VetBond (available through veterinary supply catalogs)

✔ Cortisone cream for skin irritations

✔ Quick muzzle

✔ Rectal thermometer

✔ Unflavored pediatric electrolyte (Pedialyte)

✔ Syrup of Ipecac to induce vomiting

✔ Betadine solution to clean wounds and skin irritations

✔ Bandage scissors

✔ Petroleum Jelly (Vaseline) to use with rectal thermometers and as a lubricant

✔ Mineral oil for use with certain poisons

✔ Kaolin product (Kaopectate) for diarrhea

✔ Aspirin for pain and arthritis

✔ Hydrogen peroxide to clean wounds and to induce vomiting

✔ Tweezers

✔ Your veterinarian's phone number, pager, and after-hours number

✔ An emergency veterinary hospital's phone number

✔ Local poison control center phone number

NORTHERN BREED SPORTS

Whether you have one dog or many, you can enjoy the different sled dog activities with your Northern breed. Backpacking, skijoring, and weightpulling require only one dog, although you can do the activities with multiple dogs, if you choose. Sledding or mushing requires a minimum of two dogs. Three dogs allow you to run competitively.

Which Sport Is Right for You and Your Northern Breed?

Some sports, such as backpacking and weightpulling, require a minimal amount of gear. If you already own skis and winter equipment, skijoring can be inexpensive as well. The commitment to these sports is also much less than sledding. Sledding or mushing becomes expensive in both time and equipment.

Some breed clubs have titles available for dogs that accomplish certain standards in sledding, weightpulling, and packing. Check with your national breed club to see if you can earn titles.

Whether you have one dog or many, you can enjoy the different sled dog activities with your Northern breed. This Samoyed enjoys backpacking.

Conditioning Your Northern Breed

Most housepets are overweight. To determine Yukon's condition, put your thumbs on his spine and feel the ribs with your outstretched fingers. You should be able to easily feel his spine, ribs, and rib cage. Moving your hands toward the tail, you should also be able to feel the pelvis. If you cannot feel them, Yukon is too fat for working. Your veterinarian may recommend a special low-calorie diet. If Yukon is currently exercising, you may wish to use a premium performance dog food, but simply feed him less.

Once Yukon is at his optimal weight, consider the following conditioning activities:
- ✔ Long walks and hikes
- ✔ Roadwork by using a bicycle with a special attachment for dogs
- ✔ Treadmill
- ✔ Drag training—teaching Yukon to drag a light tire behind a weightpull harness
- ✔ Agility

Yukon will also need the proper diet to work out; see the Nutrition chapter.

Backpacking/Hiking

If Yukon is healthy, free from injuries, joint problems, and bone malformations, he can certainly pack! Even healthy older dogs may pack, if you consider age and condition. Do not backpack Yukon until he is at least 18 months old. Backpacking will stress growing bones and joints and may cause irreparable damage. Ask your veterinarian when you can safely backpack your dog.

If you intend to backpack with Yukon, have your veterinarian thoroughly examine him. He may wish to inoculate Yukon against Lyme disease and start him on heartworm medication, if he is not already on it. You may also wish to discuss tick repellent and first aid kits for dogs.

Any size dog can backpack, but the usefulness of the dog depends largely on his size. Never have a dog carry more than one third of his weight, as a rule, without prior conditioning. Most dogs, when starting out, should carry

no more than 20 percent of their weight. The amount of weight depends on the breed and dog's condition. If you have any doubts, reduce the weight immediately. Serious injuries can result from too heavy a load.

Fitting the Backpack

A properly fitting backpack is crucial to your dog's comfort. It should rest over the dog's shoulders at the base of the neck. The pack should have a chest strap that clips in front of the dog's chest and a belly band that tightens underneath the ribs. The pack is too small if the bottom of the panniers is more than a couple of inches above the elbows; it is too large if the pack extends beyond the hips.

Choose Fastex-type snaps. These are easier to adjust, fasten, and release than old-style

A dog backpack and how it should fit.

Equipment Needed for Backpacking/Hiking

Yukon will need the following items for backpacking/hiking:
✔ Backpack—either with or without removable panniers.
✔ Tracking leash—a cotton webbing leash, 10–15 feet long (3–4.6 m), intended to allow the dog to forge ahead.
✔ Training collar—either a slip-type collar or martingale-type collar with limited slip. Prong or pinch collars are useful for dogs that pull hard.
✔ Collapsible water and food bowls and water containers.
✔ Dog first aid kit (see previous chapter.)
✔ Dog booties—made from cordura nylon; useful for protecting worn pads.
✔ Bags for picking up dog waste.

buckles and fasteners. Other nice features available with dog packs include

✔ lash panels or D-rings on top. This feature allows you to lash items to the top of the pack.

✔ removable panniers. This feature allows you to remove the pack and its contents, while still keeping the pack's base and straps on the dog.

✔ curved panniers that prevent the dog from bumping his elbows into the pack.

✔ ballistic nylon for durability.

✔ open mesh on top between panniers on smaller, lighter packs.

✔ reflective tape.

✔ extra pockets.

Getting Your Northern Breed Used to the Pack

Take Yukon for a walk wearing the backpack to accustom him to walking with something on his back. Fill the panniers with crumpled newspaper so he can learn how wide he will be with the pack on. Give him plenty of praise and treats as you lead him around with his pack.

Later, if Yukon is over 30 pounds, add a soup can in each pannier. Add more weight with each session until the weight equals 20 percent of Yukon's total weight.

Tip: Start slowly and with no more than 20 percent of the dog's weight for two miles (3.2 km) or less. Choose easy terrain. If Yukon shows any sign of fatigue, remove the pack, give him water and a rest. As he becomes more conditioned to packing, lengthen the hike a mile or two. Vary the terrain. Rough, hilly terrain is harder than flat, compacted trails, so shorten the mileage on more difficult hikes. Once Yukon becomes conditioned, he can carry

a third of his weight comfortably over longer distances.

Where to Pack

Choose a trail you know. Some trails are inaccessible to dogs with packs due to steep or very rugged terrain; other trails may ban dogs. Choose an easy trail with level terrain for your first hike. Make it fun. If Yukon becomes discouraged while packing, lighten the load or remove the pack. Go to a spot where you can take off the pack for a while and have fun.

Weightpulling

In weightpulling, a dog in harness pulls a sled or a cart with heavy weights for a distance of 16 feet (4.9 m). Any healthy dog is capable of weightpulling. Most dogs, even small dogs, are capable of pulling many times their weight, provided they are properly trained and are physically sound. Dogs enjoy the work and competition as much as if not more, than their owners do. They pull for the sheer enjoyment with no coercion.

There are six weight classes in the International Weight Pull Association's (IWPA) sanctioned pulls, which includes dogs under 35 pounds (15.9 kg), dogs between 35 and 60 pounds (15.9–27 kg), dogs between 60 and 80 pounds (27–36 kg), dogs between 80 and 100 pounds (36–45 kg), dogs between 100 and 120 pounds (45–54 kg), and dogs over 120 pounds (54 kg). Other sanctioning bodies may have different weight classes and rules.

If weightpulling appeals to you, be aware that your dog must be older than one year and younger than 12 years in order to compete. Other weightpulling sanctioning bodies may

Sledding or mushing requires a minimum of two dogs. Three dogs allow you to run competitively. These are Alaskan Huskies.

have different age requirements. With large breeds, owners may wish to wait until their dogs are at least 18 months. If you have a young dog, ask your veterinarian when your dog will be able to participate in weightpulls and weightpull training. For further information on weightpulling, see Information, page 92.

Equipment

Weightpulling requires very little equipment, making it an inexpensive sport. The dog must

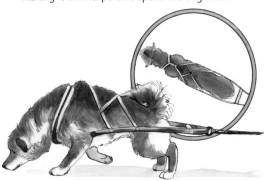

have a properly fitted weightpull harness. Most owners start training using a small tire hooked to a long chain behind the dog's tug ring. If you wish to begin with a lighter weight, screw a large eye-bolt into the top of a fence post, a 2 × 4, or a stick of firewood. You can then attach a rope or an old leash to the drag.

The Correct Weightpull Harness

Do *not* use mushing harnesses or so-called "roading" harnesses (sometimes available at pet stores). They can cause severe injury to a dog in freighting and weightpulling. The correct harness is the Siwash freighting harness available from weightpulling and mushing outfitters. This harness is heavily padded with foam or synthetic sheepskin. Like the mushing X-back harness it

A correctly fitting weightpull harness. Note the spreader bar or singletree behind the dog's rear legs that keeps the straps from interfering with the dog's pulling.

does crisscross across the back. However, unlike mushing harnesses, the harness straps do not meet at the base of the tail on top of the rump; they run the length of the dog, just below the elbow, and meet behind the dog's flank to a ring. Just behind the flank is a spreader bar or "single-tree"—a round or square half-inch dowel that holds the straps apart, enabling the dog to "dig in" with his hind legs. Do not weightpull with a harness that does not have a spreader bar.

Introducing Your Northern Breed to the Harness

Harness Yukon as described in the TIP box, How to Harness a Dog. Have treats ready and praise him to distract him from this new thing. If he tries to chew the harness, gently correct him with a *"No! No chew!"* and offer him something to chew instead.

Beginning Drag Training

Start with drag training as described in the Drag Training section of HOW-TO: Teaching Your Northern Breed to Pull, page 90. Once Yukon is comfortable with basic drag training, start with the piece of firewood or 2 × 4 with an eyebolt and hook a rope or chain to the tug ring and the other end to the eyebolt. Choose a level area, covered in dirt, without undulations. Snap a leash on Yukon's collar and lead him forward in a straight line. He should feel the weight of the drag. If the weight is not too heavy, or if he is a determined puller, he may charge through without giving the weight a thought. Use a treat to lure his head lower as he pulls so that he learns the correct form. You want his head low so that he uses his shoulders and chest to pull the weight. Praise him and give him the treat.

A Samoyed rests on the trail.

Any dog in good condition can backpack. This is a Karelian Bear Dog.

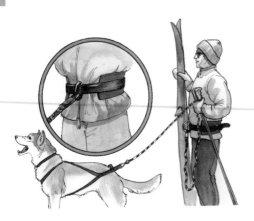

A skijoring set-up. Note the quick-release buckle on the skijoring belt.

If Yukon hesitates, use food to lure him forward. Keep it low and just a few inches out of his reach. If the weight is not too great, he should make an attempt at trying to get the treat. Praise him and give him the treat as he moves forward. Use more food to coax him—don't stop him, just give him the treat as he gains momentum. If, at any time, he cannot pull the weight or gives up, help him by pushing the weight, then praise him. Give him less weight and work with him to rebuild his confidence. Weightpulling is mostly a mental exercise for the dog. While the dog must be in good condition to pull, he must be convinced he can pull. Once Yukon shows confidence in pulling the weight, practice pulling that weight 10 starts for about 30 feet (9 m). After each pull or each two or three pulls, unhook the weight and walk him around to stretch out his muscles. With each pull, use a command to pull, such as "*Hike!*" or "*Dig!*" Train for two weeks once or twice a day.

After two weeks, Yukon should become comfortable with the drag. The next step is to switch to a loose fence post with an eyebolt. At this phase, you may want to decide whether to call him from the front or "drive" him from behind. Both have their advantages. Many dogs love coming to their owners for hugs and kisses. Other dogs love having their owners drive them from behind, feeling that this is more a team effort. Try both—no doubt one will seem more natural to you. You will also want to teach Yukon the *stay* command, if he does not know it yet. Put him on a long leash, give him the *stay* command, and have someone hold him while you take your position, either to call him or drive him. Give him a moment or two to wait and then command him to pull. Again, give him two weeks of training with the new drag.

Assuming Yukon is not a toy or small breed, your next step is to use a small tire from a compact car as a drag. Lay the tire flat on the ground. Use chains to hook the tire to Yukon's tug. Again, practice good form: head lowered, shoulders forward. As he becomes used to the weight, you may start adding additional weight. Chains or bricks added slowly will increase the drag. You will first start with the tire only. Have Yukon pull the weight for five to 10 starts for 30 feet (9 m). Then, increase the weight and practice for five to 10 starts for 25 feet (7.6 m). Increase the weight again and have Yukon pull the weight 20 feet (6.1 m) for two to five starts. The last increase in weight should be close to Yukon's maximum and he should pull only one to three times. Then, remove some weight and have Yukon pull the lower weight. The workout should consist of 20 to 35 starts with rests and walks between each start.

If at any time Yukon balks at the weight help him with it, so he can finish the pull. Reduce the weight and have him pull it. End on a positive note. Practice every day or every other day, but do not try for too much too soon.

Weightpull Competitions

Weightpull competitions are fun and exciting for both dogs and owners. The competition requires that the dogs weigh in and determine their class. You cannot use a leash, food, toys, or anything that might be considered a motivator or coercion while the dog is weight-pulling. The dog must pull the weight 16 feet (4.9 m) within one minute.

Skijoring/Pulka

In skijoring the dog pulls the owner who is on skis. In pulka, or Nordic-style mushing, the skijorer skis behind a small sled or pulk, which the dog pulls. In pulka, the towline attaches the skijorer to the dog and the sled.

If your Northern breed is healthy and over 30 pounds (13.6 kg), he can be a skijoring dog. Have your veterinarian check his hips and elbows for dysplasia before starting to skijor. With a puppy, you can began harness training and light drag training before he reaches a year, but do not have him pull you until at least a year. For more information on skijoring/pulka, see Information, page 92.

One, Two, or More?

Always start out skijoring with one dog. Once you feel comfortable with his training, you can try skijoring. Do not do this alone! Have a friend go with you who is a proficient skier or who can follow you down a trail. Choose an uncrowded, flat, wide trail or area for your first run. Put Yukon in a *stay* and

Equipment Needed for Skijoring/Pulka

✔ You should have your own ski equipment and clothing. The type of skis is strictly up to you, but many people prefer cross-country skis because they allow the owner to work behind the dog more easily.

✔ You will need a skijoring belt or harness. It can be made from leather or nylon. It should be padded for your comfort and have a quick-release snap in case you must quickly free yourself from your dog.

✔ You will need a towline and shockcord. The towline is made from spliced polyethylene rope that attaches one, two, or three dogs to the skijorer. It should be long enough to provide a safe buffer zone for Yukon in case you lose control. The shockcord, constructed from bungee, attaches to the towline and protects the dog from hard jolts.

✔ Your dog will need an X-back or H-back racing harness. These are the same harnesses used by mushers.

✔ If you intend to try pulka or Nordic-style mushing, you will need a special harness that attaches to the pulk shafts. You will also have to purchase a specially made pulk or Nordic sled. Pulks are quite expensive. If you are interested in Nordic-style mushing, you may wish to try skijoring first to see if you like it before investing in a pulk.

✔ The dog may need booties to protect his paws from snowballing and abrasive snow.

✔ You may wish to purchase a dog coat for extremely cold weather, in case your dog has a short coat.

TIP

Training on Dirt

Many mushers now use ATVs or All Terrain Vehicles for training sled teams on dirt. ATVs offer more control than carts with excellent braking and power to help teams up hills. If you choose to train with an ATV, be certain to purchase a four-wheel model. Three-wheel models are less stable and more prone to accidents.

---

have your friend hold him while you hook him up to your skijoring belt. Use the words "*Hike!*" to go and "*Whoa!*" to stop, as in prior training.

Activities will keep your Northern breed fit. While this Alaskan Klee Kai is too small to pack, he would enjoy hiking in the outdoors as much as his larger cousins.

Your first few runs should be short as you learn how to help Yukon as he tows you. You will have to worry about stopping correctly to avoid hitting him and making a smooth transition going forward. As your confidence builds, start working toward skijoring for a mile or more. Once you feel confident with your dog and his abilities—as well as your abilities—you can add a second skijor dog. Just be certain that Tasha is as well trained as Yukon and that they get along—you don't need to break up a dog fight in the middle of a trail!

Skijoring Competitions

Most skijoring competitions are sprint races between three to five miles (4.8–8 km), although there are skijoring distance races. These distance races may go 20 miles (32 km) or more. Skijor races are divided into the classes of 1-dog, 2-dog, or 3-dog skijor. These races are usually run over a weekend with two "heats." The combined time of both heats make up your final time for the race.

Mushing

The words "mushing" and "sled dogs" conjure up romantic images of a dog team traveling across the wilds of the frozen North. In this modern age, sled dog racing is a popular sport, not only in Alaska, but in the lower 48 as well.

If Yukon is healthy and over 30 pounds (13.6 kg), he can be a sled dog. Before you start mushing, your veterinarian should check Yukon's hips and elbows for dysplasia. If Yukon is a puppy, you can begin harness training and light drag training before he reaches a year, but you should not race him until at least a year.

How many dogs make a team? One dog can pull a person and sled over flat terrain, but in order to race, you must have a minimum of two dogs for a three-dog team. If you wish to run even somewhat competitively, you must have a minimum of three dogs.

Types of Racing

✔ Long-distance racing—made famous by such races as the Iditarod—are usually longer than 250 miles (402.5 km) and require more than 12 dogs.
✔ Sprint racing, a popular form of sled dog racing, is anywhere from three to 30 miles (4.8–48 km). Limited class sprint racing is measured as one mile (1.6 km) per dog; so a three-dog race will go an average of three miles (4.8 km). There are also four-, six-, eight-, and ten-dog races in the limited class. Unlimited class races tend to be 20 to 30 miles (32–48 km) long. There are usually two heats in a sprint race, run over consecutive days.
✔ Mid-distance races are anywhere from 20 to 250 miles (32–402.5 km) and usually require six, ten, or more dogs to race.
✔ Stage races are a new type of racing in which the race is run for a set number of miles each day for two to ten days. Stage races are a hybrid compromise between sprint racing and distance racing. The number of dogs depends on the race. As stage racing is relatively new, the rules are evolving.
✔ Cart racing is done with wheeled carts, rigs, or gigs on dirt. Like sprint races, cart races are

Equipment Needed

✔ Sled—either a basket sled or a toboggan sled. Basket sleds are more often used for shorter races on groomed trails because they are lighter. Toboggans are used for distance races where there is a need to carry supplies over ungroomed trails.
✔ Gangline—the line that attaches the dogs to the sled.
✔ X-back or H-back harnesses—one per dog.
✔ Sled bag—bag used for carrying equipment or an injured dog.
✔ Snowhook—hook used to anchor the sled when stopped.
✔ Snublines—an alternative method to tying off the sled.
✔ Shockcord—a thick bungee that protects the dogs from hard jolts.
✔ Booties—items used to protect the dogs' feet from abrasive snow and to prevent snowballing.
✔ Dog coats—items used to provide extra warmth in extreme conditions.

Upper sled—a basket sled, used primarily for shorter distances. Lower sled is a toboggan sled, used for heavier loads and longer distances. The bed helps it "float" in deep snow.

TIP

Mushing Equipment Terms

✔ Basket sled—a lashed sled where the bed is raised several inches off the ground. The bed is usually made from lashed pieces of wood; generally smaller and lighter than the toboggan and used for shorter distances.

✔ Bridle—a piece of line that attaches to the sled—usually to the stanchions—that the gangline hooks to.

✔ Brush bow—a heavy-duty, curved piece of polyethylene plastic or wood that attaches to the front of the sled. It provides some protection when hitting or going over obstacles.

✔ Driving bow—the "handlebar" for the musher; usually made from curved wood or polyethylene.

✔ Gangline or mainline—The center section of a tandem dog line that tuglines and necklines connect to. Gangline often is used to refer to the entire line, including mainline, tuglines, and necklines.

✔ H-back harness—a special harness that allows greater expansion of the chest. Often seen on distance dogs, this harness is for dogs that the X-back does not fit well.

✔ Neckline—the line that stretches from the gangline to connect to the dog's collar.

✔ Runners—the fixed skis of the sled.

✔ Shock cord—a piece of line fitted with a bungee, or several bungees, to help take the pounding and prevent dog's injuries; usually attached between the gangline and the sled's bridle.

✔ Snow hook—a forged, heavy piece of metal with claws at the end intended to hold a dog team in snow.

✔ Snub line—a piece of rope used to tie off the sled; sometimes has a quick-release snap.

✔ Stanchion—the main upright supports of a sled.

✔ Toboggan sled—a sled where the bed lays on the runners only a few inches from the ground. The bed is usually made from high-density plastic and is curved to provide a larger surface for ungroomed trails. Toboggans are traditionally heavier with a lower center of gravity.

✔ Tug or tug loop—a small piece of rope that connects to the back of the dog's harness where the tugline connects.

✔ Tugline—The line that stretches from the gangline or mainline to the dog's tug on his harness.

✔ X-back harness—a special racing harness design that is padded along the neck and chest. The X crosses the back, hence the name; used on both sprint and distance dogs.

usually run one mile (1.6 km) per dog. Some organizations are offering distance cart races, where the mileage may be 15 to 25 miles (24–40 km) a heat.

✔ Freight racing is a type of race where a team must pull a certain amount of weight per dog over a few miles. This type of racing is not as popular as the other types.

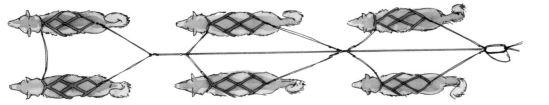

The gangline and positions. Left-most: lead dogs. Middle: point dogs are right behind the lead dogs. Other dogs in the team would be called swing dogs, such as 1st Swing, 2nd Swing, etc. Right-most: Wheel dogs are right in front of the sled.

Modern Mushing

Unlike Jack London's world of the Arctic, modern-day sled dogs receive excellent care. Dog food manufacturers and veterinary schools have made the sled dog's diet and performance the subject of extensive research. Race organizations ban the use of steroids and medications that seek to enhance performance or suppress symptoms of a serious condition. Likewise, these organizations prohibit abusive treatment of sled dogs at any race. Major sanctioning bodies such as the International Sled Dog Racing Association

(ISDRA) ban whips. In any race, the welfare of the dogs is paramount.

However, mushing is an expensive sport. Many beginners, not understanding the overall cost in time and money, quickly collect dogs, only to discover the drawbacks. These people leave the sport almost as quickly as they came in, often at the dogs' expense. Organizations such as Mush with PRIDE focus to educate novice mushers on their responsibilities as sled dog owners.

TIP

The Correct Sledding Harness

Do *not* use weightpulling harnesses or so-called "roading" harnesses (sometimes available at pet stores). Weightpull harnesses can cause severe injury to a dog when running if the dog catches his leg in the singletree (a round or square small dowel that holds the straps apart). The correct harness is either the X-back or H-back sledding harness that you can purchase from mushing outfitters. This harness is padded with foam or synthetic sheepskin. The X-back is similar to Siwash harness as it has a crisscross across the back. However, unlike freighting harnesses, the harness straps meet at the base of the tail on top of the rump and do not have a singletree.

This is a correct fitting X-back harness.

These Samoyeds love sharing the load with their owners.

Siberian Huskies in harness.

Training for Sledding

You should have Yukon trained as a lead dog, as described on page 90. Once you train him as a command lead, train your other dogs the rudiments of pulling. They should know *"Hike!"* *"Whoa!"* and *"Tighten up!"* Unless you have experienced sled dogs, add dogs very slowly. Most new dogs have difficulty with the gangline

Mushing Commands

✔ *Come Gee!* Or *Come Haw!*—Turn the team around to the right or left, respectively.
✔ *Easy*—Slow down.
✔ *Gee*—Go right.
✔ *Haw*—Go left.
✔ *Hike* or *Let's Go!* —Go forward.
✔ *Tighten up* or *Line out*—Tighten the tugline or hold the team.
✔ *Whoa*—Stop.

and quickly become tangled. If this happens, stop the team immediately and untangle it. A tangled dog can injure itself or others and the situation may lead to a dogfight. Also, never drag a dog; a dragged dog can be seriously injured or even killed.

Begin your training in the fall, when the weather turns cooler. Dogs overheat quickly in warm weather, a good rule is to not run a team when it is warmer than 50°F (10°C). In some areas, this may be prohibitive to mushing, or the dogs must be specially conditioned for the type of weather. In Alaska, for example, some dogs may overheat above 35°F (1.7°C). In some areas in the continental United States, mushers run their sled dogs in temperatures above 50 degrees but in any case, watch for signs of heat exhaustion and take frequent water breaks.

Start training by going only a half-mile every day for a week. Practice stopping and getting off

TIP

How to Harness a Dog

Harnessing a dog for sledding, skijoring, or weightpulling can be confusing for someone who has never done it before. Follow these steps to harness a dog:

1. Hold the harness by the padded neck-pieces. (They will make a circular opening).

2. Look for the padded "Y"—this is the chest piece. If the chest is a split-chest design, the "Y" may be more difficult to locate. In which case, the chest piece will always be padded. The top of the harness that lies on the dog's withers will be an "X." The lower half of the "X" will be padded; the top half will not be.

3. Hold the harness so that the two pieces of webbing that come from the bottom of the "Y," line up with the padded portion.

4. Straddle your dog. With the "Y" pointing upright, but downward, slip the harness opening over the dog's head.

5. Pull the chest piece, (the lower part of the "Y") over the chest.

6. Gently lift each front foot and slip them through each of the straps that come out of the "Y"—one strap for each leg.

7. Tug on the tug loop towards the back of the dog.

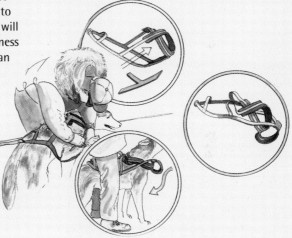

the sled or cart. (Be certain to properly tie off the sled or cart with a snubline to prevent unexpected departures.) Offer a quick treat to each of the dogs. As your dogs become used to your commands and control, they will become more reliable. Do not hook up more dogs than you can reasonably control; for most people, this is four dogs. As you gain experience, you can add dogs, provided that they are already harness-trained.

After the first week, increase to running one mile every day. As the days turn cooler and your dogs become more conditioned, you can take fewer breaks. Each week, double the mileage until you reach one mile (1.6 km) per dog in the team. If you have four dogs, by the end of a month, you should be running four miles (6 km). At that point, you can train two to four times a week until racing season.

✔ Start with a 6-foot (1.8-m) leash and a 10-foot (3-m) long line. Clip the leash to Yukon's flat collar and the long line to the tug loop at the end of his harness. Put him in a *stand-stay* with light tension on the "tug-line." Command "*Line-out*" or "*Tighten-up*" and quietly praise him if he holds the tension.

✔ If he wheels around or comes back to you, put him back in the original position. Continue to praise him for holding that position. Return him to the position if he steps out of line.

✔ Always use quiet praise, too much enthusiastic praise can cause him to come back and celebrate with you! Also, keep minimal contact as you put him back—no petting! If you pet him every time he breaks his position, he will break every time.

✔ Next, take a step forward. Yukon should move forward to keep the line tight. If he doesn't, give him the command "*Tighten up!*" If he doesn't respond, treat this as you would in the first steps of getting him to hold tension on the line. Practice taking steps forward and having him tighten up the line until he is comfortable with this lesson. Practice this five to ten minutes a day for a week.

✔ Once Yukon is used to "*Tighten up*," give him the command "*Hike!*" or "*Let's go!*" and start moving toward him. If he is confused, use the words "*Tighten up*" or you may have to point in the direction you wish to go and perhaps give him light tugs with the leash in the appropriate direction. Praise him generously for any forward movement. If he comes back to you, put him back in his *tighten up* position and work on getting him to keep the line tight.

✔ Every time Yukon steps forward, *praise him*. If he steps to the side or stops to sniff, tell him, "*No, hike!*" If you are consistent, he will learn quickly that "*Hike!*" means go forward. When you stop, use the command "*Whoa!*" Yukon should stand forward with tension on the tugline. If not, command him to tighten up. Practice for two weeks.

Once you teach Yukon these basics, try finding a tree or post to tie the "tugline" to. Practice "tighten-up" and teach him that even though he is not tied to you, he should still keep the line tight. You may wish to tie his tug to the tree, give him a tighten-up command, and then walk a few feet away, pretending to ignore him. If he breaks, put him back in the tighten-up position.

Drag Training

Attach a lightweight drag to the end of the harness. A small

Sports with Northern breeds is as old as the breeds themselves. The dogs love to work and for people who find being outdoors working as a team with their animals, there is no more exhilirating way to spend their time.

branch or piece of firewood works well, as long as it provides some drag and will clatter or bounce a bit when the dog is pulling. Put a leash on the flat collar and give him the "*Hike!*" command. Keep sessions short until Yukon's confidence builds.

If he panics with the drag, stop the training and unsnap the drag from his tug loop. Show him the drag and let him sniff it. Then work on previous exercises to give him a positive experience to end the training. Wait a few days and then try the drag again. Offer treats and praise if he makes small gains with the drag.

"Gee-Haw" Training

Teaching a dog right from left can be daunting. Mushers use the words "Gee" for right and "Haw" for left. A dog will learn "Right" and "Left" as easily as "Gee" and "Haw," so don't feel as though you have to use them. Just be consistent.

If you have only one lead dog, find a place with multiple intersections and trails and start teaching the commands there. If you live in a suburban area with plenty of intersections, this will work well. When you and Yukon approach an intersection, tell him the direction you wish to go (*"Gee"* or *"Haw"*) or straight ahead (*"Straight"* or *"On by!"*). Because Yukon will not know the command, you may find him looking back for guidance. If you have told him *"Gee!"* start tugging on the "neckline" to the right. He may resist and you may have to physically turn him to the right, but once he does go right, praise him. After the turn, stop him (tie his tug to something) and give him a treat. Be certain to stay beside him, not in front. You want him to lead out, not come to you. Practice all commands frequently. Dogs often do better with one command than another so if Yukon is better with *"Gee,"* work on *"Haw"* with some *"Gee"* commands thrown in to boost morale.

Practice commands every day for five to ten minutes for the next three weeks. If Yukon looks bored or is having difficulties with the commands, try mixing older lessons in with the new ones. Sometimes giving a dog a task he has learned that is now easy can help instill confidence when the training becomes harder. Switch training areas if you can. Spend some time playing with him, instead of just training.

After Yukon gains enough confidence with the commands, hook him up alone to the sled. If you plan to skijor, introduce him to a level area and use your skis. When you come to an intersection, give him the command. If it is *"Haw!"* for example, and he decides to go forward, secure the sled and show him where you wish to go. Do this by walking up to him on the left, clapping your hands, and calling to him or taking him by the collar and leading him to the left. Keep telling him *"Haw!"* If he is stubborn, you may have to lead him to the trail.

Once you have convinced him that going left is a good idea, stop him and give him a treat. Work with him with the sled and on foot. Change trails frequently and never take the same turns. Dogs have wonderful memories for trails and Yukon may have the turns memorized rather than learning commands.

Putting It All Together

After you are reasonably confident in Yukon's abilities to lead, you may wish to add another dog. The other dog should be familiar will pulling a sled or skijoring. If Tasha is unfamiliar with sledding, first work on *"Hike"*, *"Whoa"*, and *"Tighten up"* with her. When you add another dog, keep Yukon's mind on leading, not on playing or investigating. Tasha may do better behind Yukon, rather than in tandem. Try different positions to see which works best.

Organizations

The American Kennel Club
5580 Centerview Drive
Suite 200
Raleigh, NC 27606
Phone: (919) 233-9767
Fax: (919) 233-3740
E-mail: *info@akc.org*
Web site: *www.akc.org*

Canine Eye Registration Foundation
Department of Veterinary Clinical Science
School of Veterinary Medicine
Purdue University
West Lafayette, IN 47907
Phone: (765) 494-8179
Fax: (765) 494-9981
Web site: *http://www.vet.purdue.edu/~yshen/
cerf.html*

International Sled Dog Racing Association
HC 86 Box 3390
Merrifield, MN 56465
Phone: (218) 765-4297
Fax: (218) 765-3246
E-mail: *dsteele@brainerd.net*
Web site: *www.isdra.org*

Mush With PRIDE
Box 84915
Fairbanks, AK 99708-4915

Orthopedic Foundation for Animals
2300 Nifong Boulevard
Columbia, MO 65201
Phone: (314) 442-0418
Web site: *www.offa.org*

United Kennel Club (UKC)
100 East Kilgore Road
Kalamazoo, MI 49001-5593
http://www.ukcdogs.com/

Periodicals
Dog Fancy Magazine
PO Box 6050
Mission Viejo, CA 92690

Dog and Driver
(See ISDRA)

Dog World
29 N. Wacker Drive
Chicago, IL 60606

Mushing Magazine
PO Box 149
Ester, AK 99725-0149

Books
Alderton, David. *The Dog Care Manual.* Hauppauge, New York: Barron's Educational Series, 1986.
American Kennel Club. *The Complete Dog Book, 19th Edition Revised.* New York: Howell Book House, 1997.
Baer, Ted. *Communicating with Your Dog.* Hauppauge, New York: Barron's Educational Series, 1989.
Bailey, Gwen. *The Well-Behaved Dog.* Hauppauge, New York: Barron's Educational Series, 1998.
Benjamin, Carol Lea. *Second-Hand Dog.* New York: Howell Book House, 1988.
Bonham, Margaret H. *An Introduction to Dog Agility.* Hauppauge, New York: Barron's Educational Series, 2000.
Carlson, Delbert G. and James M. Giffin, M.D. *The Dog Owner's Home Veterinary Handbook.* New York: Howell Book House, 1992.

Coffman, Howard D. *The Dry Dog Food Reference*. Nashua, New Hampshire: Pig Dog Press, 1995.

Collins, Donald R. *The Collins Guide to Dog Nutrition*. New York: Howell Book House, 1987.

Collins, Miki and Julie. *Dog Driver: A Guide for the Serious Musher*. Loveland, Colorado: Alpine Publications, 1991.

Coppinger, Lorna. *The World of Sled Dogs*. New York: Howell Book House, 1977.

Elliot, Rachel Page. *The New Dogsteps*. New York: Howell Book House, 1984.

Fishback, Lee. *Training Lead Dogs*. Nunica, Michigan: Tun-Dra, 1978.

Gilbert, Edward M. Jr., and Thelma R. Brown. *K-9 Structure and Terminology*. New York: Howell Book House, 1995.

Hinchcliff, Kenneth W., Gregory A. Reinhart, Arleigh J. Reynolds. *Performance Dog Nutrition*. Dayton, Ohio: The Iams Company, 1999.

Holst, Phyllis A. *Canine Reproduction, A Breeder's Guide*. Loveland, Colorado: Alpine Publications, 1985.

Hoe-Raitto, Mari and Carol Kaynor. *Skijor with Your Dog*. Fairbanks, Alaska: OK Publishing, 1991.

James, Ruth B. *The Dog Repair Book*. Mills, Wyoming: Alpine Press, 1990.

Klever, Ulrich. *The Complete Book of Dog Care*. Hauppauge, New York: Barron's Educational Series, 1989.

LaBelle, Charlene. *A Guide to Backpacking with Your Dog*. Loveland, Colorado: Alpine Publications, 1993.

Levorsen, Bella, editor. *Mush! A Beginner's Manual of Sled Dog Training*. Westmoreland, New York: Arner Publications, 1976.

Merck and Co. *The Merck Veterinary Manual*. Seventh Edition. Whitehouse Station, New Jerset: Merck and Co, Inc., 1991.

Papurt, M. L. *Saved! A Guide to Success with Your Shelter Dog*. Hauppauge, New York: Barron's Educational Series, 1997.

In Alaska and other northern areas, sled dogs are tied out because deep snow makes kennels impractical. This Siberian Husky is waiting to join the team at a race.

Pryor, Karen. *Don't Shoot the Dog! The New Art of Teaching and Training*. New York: Bantam Doubleday Dell, 1999.

Ralston Purina Company. *Purina's Complete Guide to Nutrition, Care, and Health for your Dog and Cat*. St. Louis, Missouri: Ralston Purina Company.

Rice, Dan. *The Complete Book of Dog Breeding*. Hauppauge, New York: Barron's Educational Series, 1996.

Smith, Cheryl S. *Pudgy Pooch, Picky Pooch*. Hauppauge, New York: Barron's Educational Series, 1998.

Smith, Cheryl S. and Stephanie J. Tauton. *The Trick is in the Training*. Hauppauge, New York: Barron's Educational Series, 1998.

Streitferdt, Uwe. *Healthy Dog, Happy Dog*. Hauppauge, New York: Barron's Educational Series, 1994.

Dedication

To the Johnson family: Sue, Sandy, Joe, Jerry, assorted Alaskan Malamutes, one Border Collie and one Golden Retriever for their gracious hospitality shown during the High Meadow fire. That is what true friends are for. And for Larry, as always.

About the Author

Margaret H. "Maggie" Bonham is a freelance writer and winner of the coveted Dog Writers Association of America's "Maxwell Award". She is the author of five books, including *Northern Breeds*. She trains and races Alaskan Husky sled dogs and raises Alaskan Malamutes in Colorado. She is also the president of Canine Backpackers Association; a group dedicated to hiking and packing with dogs.

Photo Credits

Kent and Donna Dannen: 3, 4, 8, 9, 12 (left), 13 (left), 16 (left), 21 (bottom left and right), 24, 25, 28, 40, 44, 48, 49, 53, 56, 61 (bottom), 64, 69, 72, 76, 81 (top), 84, 88, 93. Courtesy Sylvia Feder: 12 (right), Tara Darling: 13 (right), 16 (right), 17, 20 (top left, bottom), 21 (top left and right), 32, 52, 60, 61 (top), 68, 73, 80, 81 (bottom). Courtesy Elisabet Stacy-Hurley: 20 (right), Connie Summers: 33.

Cover Photos

All cover photos by Kent and Donna Dannen except front cover lower left by Tara Darling.

Important Note

This book is concerned with selecting, keeping, and raising any of the Northern breed dogs. The publisher and the author think it is important to point out that the advice and information for Northern breeds maintenance applies to healthy, normally developed animals. Anyone who acquires an adult dog or one from an animal shelter must consider that the animal may have behavioral problems and may, for example, bite without any visible provocation. Such anxiety biters are dangerous for the owner as well as the general public.

Caution is further advised in the association of children with dogs, in meetings with other dogs, and in exercising the dog without a leash.

Acknowledgments

The author would like to acknowledge the following people for their help and guidance: Larry Bonham, Sue Johnson, Charlene LaBelle, Susan Conant, Annette Stumf, DVM, Scott Chesney. A special thanks to Seymour Weiss, editor of *Northern Breeds* and Deborah Schneider of the Gelfman-Schneider Agency.

All inquiries should be addressed to:
Barron's Educational Series, Inc.
250 Wireless Boulevard
Hauppauge, NY 11788
http://www.barronseduc.com

International Standard Book No. 0-7641-1733-5

Library of Congress Catalog Card No. 2001018418

Library of Congress Cataloging-in-Publication Data
Bonham, Margaret H.
   Northern breeds / by Margaret H. Bonham.
      p. cm. — (Complete pet owner's manual series)
   Includes bibliographical references (p.).
   ISBN 0-7641-1733-5
   1. Northern breed dogs. I. Title. II. Complete pet owner's manual.

SF429.N57B66   2001
636.7'1–dc21   2001018418

Printed in Hong Kong

9 8 7 6 5 4 3 2 1